Past Masters
General Editor   Keith Thomas

Ruskin

Past Masters

AQUINAS Anthony Kenny
ARISTOTLE Jonathan Barnes
BACH Denis Arnold
FRANCIS BACON Anthony Quinton
BAYLE Elisabeth Labrousse
BERKELEY J. O. Urmson
THE BUDDHA Michael Carrithers
BURKE C. B. Macpherson
CARLYLE A. L. Le Quesne
CHAUCER George Kane
CLAUSEWITZ Michael Howard
COBBETT Raymond Williams
COLERIDGE Richard Holmes
CONFUCIUS Raymond Dawson
DANTE George Holmes
DARWIN Jonathan Howard
DIDEROT Peter France
GEORGE ELIOT Rosemary Ashton
ENGELS Terrell Carver
GALILEO Stillman Drake
GIBBON J. W. Burrow
GOETHE T. J. Reed
HEGEL Peter Singer

HOMER Jasper Griffin
HUME A. J. Ayer
JESUS Humphrey Carpenter
KANT Roger Scruton
LAMARCK L. J. Jordanova
LEIBNIZ G. MacDonald Ross
LOCKE John Dunn
MACHIAVELLI Quentin Skinner
MARX Peter Singer
MENDEL Vitezslav Orel
MONTAIGNE Peter Burke
THOMAS MORE Anthony Kenny
WILLIAM MORRIS Peter Stansky
MUHAMMAD Michael Cook
NEWMAN Owen Chadwick
PASCAL Alban Krailsheimer
PETRARCH Nicholas Mann
PLATO R. M. Hare
PROUST Derwent May
RUSKIN George P. Landow
ADAM SMITH D. D. Raphael
TOLSTOY Henry Gifford
WYCLIF Anthony Kenny

Forthcoming

AUGUSTINE Henry Chadwick
BAGEHOT Colin Matthew
BERGSON Leszek Kolakowski
JOSEPH BUTLER R. G. Frey
CERVANTES P. E. Russell
COPERNICUS Owen Gingerich
DESCARTES Tom Sorell
DISRAELI John Vincent
ERASMUS John McConica
GODWIN Alan Ryan
HERZEN Aileen Kelly
JEFFERSON Jack P. Greene
JOHNSON Pat Rogers
KIERKEGAARD Patrick Gardiner

LEONARDO E. H. Gombrich
LINNAEUS W. T. Stearn
MILL William Thomas
MONTESQUIEU Judith Shklar
NEWTON P. M. Rattansi
ROUSSEAU Robert Wokler
RUSSELL John G. Slater
SHAKESPEARE Germaine Greer
SOCRATES Bernard Williams
SPINOZA Roger Scruton
VICO Peter Burke
VIRGIL Jasper Griffin

and others

George P. Landow

Ruskin

Oxford New York
OXFORD UNIVERSITY PRESS
1985

Oxford University Press, Walton Street, Oxford OX2 6DP

London New York Toronto
Delhi Bombay Calcutta Madras Karachi
Kuala Lumpur Singapore Hong Kong Tokyo
Nairobi Dar es Salaam Cape Town
Melbourne Auckland

and associated companies in
Beirut Berlin Ibadan Mexico City Nicosia

Oxford is a trade mark of Oxford University Press

First published 1985 as an Oxford University Press paperback
and simultaneously in a hardback edition

British Library Cataloguing in Publication Data

Landow, George P.
Ruskin. — (Past masters)
1. Ruskin, John — Criticism and interpretation
I. Title II. Series
828'.809 PR5264
ISBN 0–19–287604–X
ISBN 0–19–287603–1 Pbk

Set by Grove Graphics
Printed in Great Britain by
St. Edmundsbury Press Ltd.
Bury St. Edmunds, Suffolk

Preface

Like all Ruskin's readers, I owe a great debt of gratitude to E. T. Cook and Alexander Wedderburn, the editors of the Library Edition, who have done so much to advance the cause of Ruskin studies. My own particular study of Ruskin began several decades ago in a seminar taught by Professor E. D. H. Johnson of Princeton University, and only he knows how much I owe to his generous advice and guidance. John L. Bradley, upon whose 'Calendar' from *An Introduction to Ruskin* (Boston, 1971) I have based my 'Ruskin Chronology', has always been wonderfully kind and encouraging, and I am deeply grateful to him and to Paul Sawyer, who kindly provided me with a manuscript copy of his important book on Ruskin before its publication. I would also like to thank John D. Rosenberg, Van Akin Burd, James Dearden, Elizabeth K. Helsinger, and all other Ruskinians whose work has proved so important to the development of the ideas in this volume.

Jay Charles Rosenthal, Shoshana M. Landow, Noah M. Landow, and David Cody helped me read the proofs, and I would like to thank them for their assistance. My wife, Ruth M. Landow, copy-edited the book in manuscript and is responsible for much of the smoothness or clarity it may possess.

For Philip and Shirley Macktez

Contents

Note on references

All quotations from the writings of John Ruskin are taken from the *Works*, Library Edition, edited in thirty-nine volumes by E. T. Cook and Alexander Wedderburn (George Allen, London, 1903–12). The Arabic numerals in parentheses refer to volume and page numbers.

Prologue: Ruskin's life

John Ruskin was born on 8 February 1819 at 54 Hunter Street, London, the only child of Margaret and John James Ruskin. His father, a prosperous, self-made man who was a founding partner of Pedro Domecq sherries, collected art and encouraged his son's literary activities, while his mother, a devout evangelical Protestant, early dedicated her son to the service of God and devoutly wished him to become an Anglican bishop. Ruskin, who received his education at home until the age of twelve, rarely associated with other children and had few toys. During his sixth year he accompanied his parents on the first of many annual tours of the Continent. Encouraged by his father, he published his first poem, 'On Skiddaw and Derwent Water', at the age of eleven, and four years later his first prose work, an article on the waters of the Rhine.

In 1836, the year he matriculated as a gentleman-commoner at Christ Church, Oxford, he wrote a pamphlet defending the painter Turner against the periodical critics, but at the artist's request he did not publish it. While at Oxford (where his mother had accompanied him) Ruskin associated largely with a wealthy and often rowdy set but continued to publish poetry and criticism; and in 1839 he won the Oxford Newdigate Prize for poetry. The next year, however, suspected consumption led him to interrupt his studies and travel, and he did not receive his degree until 1842, when he abandoned the idea of entering the ministry. This same year he began the first volume of *Modern Painters* after reviewers of the annual Royal Academy exhibition had again savagely treated Turner's works, and in 1846, after making his first trip abroad without his parents, he published the second volume, which discussed his theories of beauty and imagination within the context of figural as well as landscape painting.

On 10 April 1848 Ruskin married Euphemia Chalmers Gray, and the next year he published *The Seven Lamps of Architecture*, after which he and Effie set out for Venice. In 1850 he published *The King of the Golden River*, which he had written for Effie nine years before, and a volume of poetry, and in the following year, during which Turner died and Ruskin made the acquaintance of the Pre-Raphaelites, the first volume of *The Stones of Venice*. The final two volumes appeared in 1853, the summer of which saw Millais, Ruskin, and Effie together in Scotland, where the artist painted Ruskin's portrait. The next year his wife left him and had their marriage annulled on grounds of non-consummation, after which she later married Millais. During this difficult year, Ruskin defended the Pre-Raphaelites, became close to Rossetti, and taught at the Working Men's College.

In 1855 Ruskin began *Academy Notes*, his reviews of the annual exhibition, and the following year, in the course of which he became acquainted with the man who later became his close friend, the American Charles Eliot Norton, he published the third and fourth volumes of *Modern Painters* and *The Harbours of England*. He continued his immense productivity during the next four years, producing *The Elements of Drawing* and *The Political Economy of Art* in 1857, *The Elements of Perspective* and *The Two Paths* in 1859, and the fifth volume of *Modern Painters* and the periodical version of *Unto This Last* in 1860. During 1858, in the midst of this productive period, Ruskin decisively abandoned the evangelical Protestantism which had so shaped his ideas and attitudes, and he also met Rose La Touche, a young Irish Protestant girl with whom he was later to fall deeply and tragically in love.

Throughout the 1860s Ruskin continued writing and lecturing on social and political economy, art, and myth, and during this decade he produced the *Fraser's Magazine* 'Essays on Political Economy' (1862–3; revised as *Munera Pulveris*, 1872), *Sesame and Lilies* (1865), *The Crown of Wild Olive* (1866), *The Ethics of the Dust* (1866), *Time and Tide*, and *The*

Queen of the Air (1869), his study of Greek myth. The next decade, which begins with his delivery of the inaugural lecture at Oxford as Slade Professor of Fine Art in February 1870, saw the beginning of *Fors Clavigera*, a series of letters to the working men of England, and various works on art and popularized science. His father had died in 1864 and his mother in 1871 at the age of ninety. In 1875 Rose la Touche died insane, and three years later Ruskin suffered his first attack of mental illness and was unable to testify during the Whistler trial when the artist sued him for libel. In 1880 Ruskin resigned his Oxford Professorship, suffering further attacks of madness in 1881 and 1882; but after his recovery he was re-elected to the Slade Professorship in 1883 and delivered the lectures later published as *The Art of England* (1884). In 1885 he began *Praeterita*, his autobiography, which appeared intermittently in parts until 1889, but he became increasingly ill, and Joanna Severn, his cousin and heir, had to bring him home from an 1888 trip to the Continent. He died on 20 January 1900 at Brantwood, his home near Coniston Water.

Introduction

Ruskin, the great Victorian critic of art and society, had an enormous influence on his age and our own. Like so many Victorians, he had astonishing energy, for while carrying on a voluminous correspondence and painting a large body of superb water-colours, he published poetry, a children's fantasy, and books and essays on geology, botany, church politics, political economy, painting, sculpture, literature, architecture, art education, myth, and aesthetics. He had great influence on both the nineteenth-century Gothic Revival and the twentieth-century functionalist reaction against all such revivalist styles in architecture and design. A great and successful propagandist for the arts, he did much both to popularize high art and to bring it to the masses. Ruskin, who strove to remove the boundaries between fine and applied arts, provided a major inspiration for the Arts and Crafts Movement. A brilliant theorist and practical critic of realism, he also contributed the finest nineteenth-century discussions of fantasy, the grotesque, and pictorial symbolism. A master of myth criticism, traditional iconology, and *explication du texte*, Ruskin also provides one of the few nineteenth-century instances of a writer concerned with compositional analyses and other formal criticism. His extraordinary range of taste, interests, and sympathy allowed him to discuss with perceptive enthusiasm both Turner's more traditional works and his later proto-expressionist ones, and he similarly defended (and created a taste for) painting by the English Pre-Raphaelites, Italian Primitives, and sixteenth-century Venetians. Although he was a great student of the past and past traditions, he also saw the role of the critic as having primary relevance to the present. Unlike Matthew Arnold, who during one of the great ages of English literature assured his contemporaries that they could not create major imaginative work, Ruskin perceived that they had already done so and daringly discussed Tennyson, Browning, Dickens, and others within the context of the great traditions of Western literature and art – traditions that his own writings did so much to define. In an age of great prose stylists, he was a master of many styles, perhaps the most notable of which appears in his famous passages of word-painting.

Ruskin's writings on the arts influenced not only singularly earnest Victorians, such as William Morris, William Holman Hunt, J. W. Inchbold, and a host of others, but also very different men like Walter Pater, Oscar Wilde, and William Butler Yeats. His writings on design and truth to materials had an immense influence on British, European, and American architecture and industrial design. One finds the impress of his thought in many unexpected places – in, for example, the novels and travel writings of D. H. Lawrence, works that reveal the influence of both Ruskin's art and his social criticism as well as his word-painting.

For all the attention he paid to individual works of art and their traditions, which concentration makes Ruskin the preeminent art and literary critic of the Victorian age, he also urged that we must perceive art within its social, economic, and political contexts. Indeed, as Arnold Hauser points out in *The Social History of Art* (1952):

> There has never been such a clear awareness of the organic relationship between art and life as since Ruskin. He was indubitably the first to interpret the decline of art and taste as the sign of general cultural crisis, and to express the basic, and even today not sufficiently appreciated, principle that the conditions under which men live must first be changed, if their sense of beauty and their comprehension of art are to be awakened . . . Ruskin was also the first person in England to emphasize the fact that art is a public concern and that no nation can neglect it without endangering its social existence. He was, finally, the first to proclaim the

gospel that art is not the privilege of artists, connoisseurs and the educated classes, but is part of every man's inheritance and estate ... Ruskin attributed the decay of art to the fact that the modern factory, with its mechanical mode of production and division of labour, prevents a genuine relationship between the worker and his work, that is to say, it crushes out the spiritual element and estranges the producer from the product of his hands ... [He] recalled his contemporaries to the charms of solid, careful craftsmanship as opposed to the spurious materials, senseless forms and crude, cheap execution of Victorian products. His influence was extraordinary, almost beyond description ... The purposefulness and solidity of modern architecture and industrial art are very largely the result of Ruskin's endeavours and doctrines.

Ruskin's awareness of the socio-political dimensions of art, architecture, and literature led to his writings on political economy, and reading these works changed the lives of men as different as William Morris and Mahatma Gandhi. Indeed, a survey of the first Parliament in which the British Labour Party gained seats revealed that Ruskin's *Unto This Last* had a greater influence upon its members than *Das Kapital*, and recent historians have credited him with major contributions to modern theories of the Welfare State, consumerism, and economics.

Ruskin arrived on the Victorian scene with his interpretations of art and society at precisely the right time, for he challenged the standards of the art establishment when a large number of newly rich industrialists and members of the middle class began to concern themselves with cultural issues. Because he made claims for art in the language his audience was accustomed to hear the evangelical clergy employ, these claims had particular appeal to evangelicals within and without the Church of England who formed the large majority of believers during most of the Victorian age. Similarly, Ruskin's position outside the artistic establishment, like his polemical tone, evangelical vocabulary, and Scripture citation, struck the right note with members of the rising middle class, who welcomed Ruskin's vision of an alternative form of high culture superior to that possessed by the aristocracy and older artistic establishment.

Ruskin also came forward at a particularly interesting time in the history of critical theory. Like Sir Joshua Reynolds and many other defenders of the art of painting in the West, he tried to gain prestige for visual art by coupling it with her more honoured sister, literature. Unlike most advocates of sister-arts theories, however, Ruskin did not argue that painting and poetry are allied arts because they both imitate reality. Rather, writing as an heir to the Romantic tradition, he urged that both are arts that express the emotions and imaginations of the artist. According to the Romantic conception of the poet which Ruskin learnt from Wordsworth, the poet sensitively experiences the world of man and nature and then expresses this emotional reaction to create his art. When Ruskin thus yoked a Romantic view of poetry with a Neoclassical conception of painting in creating his sister-arts theory, he characteristically refused to relinquish any aspect of the arts. Like the Neoclassical theorist, he concerned himself with the effects of art upon the audience; and like the Romantic theorist, who concentrated upon the artist's emotions and imagination, he emphasized the sincerity, originality, and intensity of great art and literature. Ruskin's Victorian aesthetic thus maintains an equal emphasis upon subjective and objective, Neoclassical and Romantic. Such richness, such eclecticism, and such willingness to confront difficult problems rather than settle for easy, more elegant solutions all characterize Ruskin's thought.

A particularly useful way into the thirty-nine massive volumes that constitute the Library Edition of Ruskin's works is provided by the recognition that throughout his career he wrote as an interpreter, an exegete. For Ruskin the act of interpretation, which leads into many fields of human experience, produces readings not only of paintings, poems, and buildings but also of contemporary phenomena, such as storm clouds and the discontent of the working classes. Whether explaining Turner's art in *Modern Painters*, the significance of an iron pub railing in *The Crown of Wild Olive*, or the nature of true wealth in *Unto This Last*, he interprets the nature and meaning of matters that he believed the British public needed to understand.

Before we look at the way Ruskin's interpretative projects form and inform his entire career, we should glance briefly at a few of his major works, for it is in the context of their varying purposes and procedures that his drive to interpret took shape and gradually evolved. *Modern Painters*, Volume I (1843), the first of these major works, opens with a brief explanation of his conceptions of power, imitation, truth, beauty, and relation in art, after which it proceeds to defend Turner against reviewers' charges that his paintings were 'unlike nature'. Summoning work after work of the old masters, he shows that this modern painter has a wider, as well as a more exact, knowledge of visible fact than any of his predecessors. He takes his opponents on their own ground and therefore demonstrates 'by thorough investigation of actual facts, that Turner *is* like nature, and paints more of nature than any man who ever lived' (3.52). Ruskin discusses general truths, by which he means tone, colour, chiaroscuro, and perspective, and then evinces the range and accuracy of Turner's representations of plants, trees, sky, earth, and water. Moving beyond its polemical origin, *Modern Painters* thus becomes a tour through nature and art conducted by a man whose eyes see and whose mind understands the phenomena of an infinitely rich natural world.

The second volume of *Modern Painters* (1846) contains both Ruskin's theories of imagination and his theocentric system of aesthetics by which he explains the nature of beauty and demonstrates its importance in human life. He combines a Coleridgean theory of imagination (which he seems to have derived indirectly by way of Leigh Hunt) with evangelical conceptions of biblical prophecy and divine inspiration. Beauty 'is either the record of conscience, written in things external, or it is a symbolizing of Divine attributes in matter, or it is the felicity of living things, or the perfect fulfilment of their duties and functions. In all cases it is something Divine' (4.210). All beauty, if properly regarded, is theophany, the revelation of God. Contemplating beauty, like contemplating the Bible, God's other revelation, is a moral and religious act.

Like much of his writing on the arts, his theories of the beautiful embody a sister-arts aesthetic and as such draw upon both Neoclassical and Romantic positions. Thus his theories of Typical (or symbolic) Beauty, which emphasize objectively existing qualities in the beautiful object, derive from Neo-classical and earlier notions that beauty is created by unity amid variety, symmetry, proportion, and other forms of chiefly visual order. In creating this Apollonian, classical aesthetic of order, Ruskin draws upon Aristotle's *Nicomachean Ethics* and the writings of Addison, Pope, Johnson, and Reynolds. In contrast, his notion of Vital Beauty, the beauty of living things, emphasizes subjective states and feelings in the spectator and derives from the Romantic poets, chiefly Wordsworth, and those eighteenth-century philosophers whose ideas of sympathy and sympathetic imagination prepared the way for Romanticism; that is, Adam Smith, David Hume, and Dugald Stewart. Ruskin, in other words, creates a Victorian aesthetic by fusing Neoclassical, Romantic, and Christian conceptions of man and his world.

Before completing *Modern Painters*, Ruskin wrote *The Seven Lamps of Architecture* (1849), another work with a heavily evangelical flavour. Despite Ruskin's turn from painting to what he termed 'the distinctly political art of architecture', *The Seven Lamps* has more in common with the second volume of *Modern Painters* than with any of his other works. Like the first two volumes of *Modern Painters*, to which it directs the reader, *The Seven Lamps of Architecture* urges that beauty and design 'are not beautiful *because* they are copied from nature; only it is out of the power of man to conceive beauty without her aid' (8.141). Furthermore, he set out to win evangelical approval of the Gothic, which was generally associated with High Church Anglicans and Roman Catholics – with the Camden and Ecclesiological Societies and with Augustus Welby Northmore Pugin. Ruskin draws upon commonplace evangelical typological interpretations of the Book of Leviticus to convince his Protestant audience that God intended man to lavish time, energy, and money upon church architecture. He similarly sounds the note of the evangelical sermon when he pleads for truth to materials in architectural construction. This note has had enormous effect on the modern world. Although Ruskin was not the only Victorian to emphasize truth to materials, he received a far wider hearing for his ideas than contemporaries who addressed their ideas only to the architectural fraternity, and architects and architectural historians alike credit him with providing the initial inspiration of much twentieth-century architecture and design.

Although self-consciously relating his comments on architecture to those expressed in his earlier volumes, Ruskin none the less sounds a new note by emphasizing the importance of communal art and creation. Furthermore, he also wants to grant the individual workman the position, independence, and pleasures of the Romantic artist. Therefore, when one considers the vitality of architecture, 'the right question to ask, respecting all ornament, is simply this: Was it done with enjoyment – was the carver happy while he was about it?' (8.218) These last two points again have done much to shape our art and design in the twentieth century, for they have influenced our cities, homes, furnishings, and utensils – the things we see and touch in everyday life. This emphasis, which inspired William Morris, the Arts and Crafts Movement, and the Bauhaus, has, like Ruskin's drawing treatises and other similar writings, also shaped our conceptions of education, leisure activity, and the status of the craftsman.

The Seven Lamps of Architecture has shaped our surroundings in yet another important way. Since Ruskin believed both that architecture is an inheritance one generation passes on to another and also that it is the embodiment of the society that built it, he tried to convince his readers to build solidly for future generations. These beliefs, like his protests throughout his work against the destruction of old buildings, stimulated the founding of English and foreign societies for architectural preservation; similarly, his conviction that those alive today are stewards, rather than owners, of works of art was a major source of the museum movement.

After completing the *The Seven Lamps of Architecture*, Ruskin turned to *The Stones of Venice*, which combines the study of architecture with a cultural history, religious polemic, and political tract. Like *The Seven Lamps, The Stones of Venice* discusses (and defends) Gothic architecture, but it moves beyond the earlier work's abstract treatment both because it devotes considerable space to the details of architectural construction and also because it places architecture within its social, political, and moral, as well as its religious context. Indeed, as Ruskin explains in its opening pages, he pays such close attention to this once powerful city because the 'arts of Venice' provide firm evidence 'that the decline of her political prosperity was exactly coincident with that of domestic and individual religion' (9.23), and it is this lesson he wishes to bring home to his Victorian audience. The first volume opens, therefore, with Ruskin sounding the prophet's note as he underlines the connections between cursed nations of the past and contemporary England:

> Since first the dominion of men was asserted over the ocean, three thrones, of mark beyond all others, have been set upon its sands: the thrones of Tyre, Venice, and England. Of the First of these great powers only the memory remains; of the Second, the ruin; the Third, which inherits their greatness, if it forget their example, may be led through prouder eminence to less pitied destruction . . .
>
> I would endeavour to . . . record, as far as I may, the warning which seems to me to be uttered by every one of the fast-gaining waves, that beat like passing bells, against the STONES OF VENICE. (9.17)

He states his goals for the entire work in this first chapter, after which he uses the volume's remaining twenty-nine to set forth a theory of architectural construction with individual chapters on the wall cornice, the capital, the roof, and so on.

Since Ruskin believes that the signs of Venetian spiritual decline appear in the city's movement from Gothic to Renaissance architectural styles, the following two volumes, *The Sea Stories* and *The Fall* (both 1853), examine the growth of the city-state and the significance of its major buildings, particularly St. Mark's and the Ducal palace. 'The Nature of Gothic', which provides the ideological core of *The Stones of Venice*, appears in the second volume and argues that because the Gothic style permits and even demands the freedom, individuality, and spontaneity of its workers, it both represents a finer, more moral society and means of production and also results in greater architecture than does the Renaissance style, which enslaves the working man. These discussions of architectural style thus lead directly to an attack on the class system and its effects. Ruskin, who has already begun to develop his consumerist ethic, focuses upon the dehumanizing conditions of modern work and urges that no one purchase goods, such as glass beads or Renaissance ornament, the production of which dehumanizes men. Ruskin the interpreter of art and Ruskin the interpreter of society here merge – or, rather, appear as one man with the same project – when he points out that his readers never have 'the idea of reading a building as we would read Milton or Dante, and getting the same kind of delight out of the stones as out of the stanzas' (10.206), because architecture produced in the dehumanizing, unmeaning contemporary way fails the people who use it just as it fails those who build it. In other words, a society that enslaves its workers in demeaning, dehumanizing work finds itself demeaned and dehumanized by the buildings they produce. These buildings, which stand as an emblematic self-indictment of the spiritual poverty at the society's core, further harm its members, rich or poor, by starving their imaginations and sensibility – faculties that Ruskin believes

12

lie at the heart of a healthy, happy, full human life.

When he resumed *Modern Painters* (1856) with the publication of Volumes III and IV, Ruskin had to solve problems raised by his earlier inclusion of Italian Renaissance art. Volume III, the central volume and probably the richest of the five, again advances a Romantic theory of painting, and all the concerns of Romanticism are here – the nature of the artist, the importance of external nature, and the role of imagination, emotion, and detail in art. The first section defines the nature of great art in order to remove apparent contradictions between the first and the second volumes which he had created by praising Giotto and Fra Angelico in Volume II. In particular, his praise of Italian Primitives seems inconsistent with his earlier demands that paintings should display a detailed knowledge of external nature. Ruskin solves the difficulty by explaining that he divides 'the art of Christian times into two great masses – Symbolic and Imitative' (5.262), and he explains that his demands for accurate representation of the external world refer only to imitative art.

Ruskin then examines the nature of greatness in art and dismisses Reynolds's Neoclassical theory that a grand style is based on the imitation of *la belle nature*, or nature idealized according to certain rules. Writing with a Romantic distrust of prescriptive rules, he offers a formula for greatness that is essentially a psychological portrait of the artist since it is based on four elements: noble subject (which the artist must instinctively love), love of beauty, sincerity, and imaginative treatment.

His discussion of the rise of landscape painting, Ruskin's second major concern in this volume, was also demanded by his somewhat unexpected inclusion of Italian art. Having begun a defence of Turner, a master of landscape, he had been diverted to other forms of painting; in order to make his way back to Turner, Ruskin felt obliged to inform his reader why landscape art had arisen at all. Classical, medieval, and modern attitudes towards external nature are considered in order to explain the origin of landscape feeling, which he argues is a peculiarly modern development and one part of a more general 'romantic love of beauty, forced to seek in history, and in external nature, the satisfaction it cannot find in ordinary life' (5.326).

In this context Ruskin introduces his famous critical concept of the Pathetic (or emotional) Fallacy, the presence of which separates Romantic and later work from the creations of Homer and Dante. According to Ruskin, the modern poet's expressionistic distortions of reality successfully communicate a subjective or phenomenological view of the world at the expense of that balanced world-view which characterizes writers of the absolute first rank. As he points out, poets and novelists who employ the emotional distortions of the Pathetic Fallacy to dramatize the mental states and experiences of a character or first-person narrator make proper use of this technique, but when an author speaking in his own person presents a distorted view of the world, he produces an essentially unbalanced (and characteristically Romantic) literature.

The fourth volume, published the same year as the third, opens with a discussion of the Turnerian picturesque and of the picturesque in general, which are the aesthetic categories specifically related to the growth of landscape art. After sections on the geology of mountain form, the volume closes with an examination of the influence of a mountain environment on the lives of men.

The fifth volume (1860) begins with sections on the beauty of leaves and clouds that are second journeys through ground covered in the first volume. Next follows a discussion of formal relation, or composition. 'Composition may best be defined as the help of everything in the picture by everything else' (7.205). This notion of help is central to Ruskin's theory of art, as it was to be in his theories of political economy, and he dwells on it at length, telling the reader that the 'highest and first law of the universe − and the other name of life, is, therefore, "help" ' (7.207). Composition, then, is the creation of an organic interrelationship between the formal elements of a work of art.

Ruskin then demonstrates, by brilliant analyses of Turner's pictorial compositions, that this artist was a master of this aspect of pictorial art.

The relation of art to life, one of Ruskin's most important interests throughout *Modern Painters* and his works on architecture, provides the heart of his section 'Invention Spiritual'. He suggests that he has begun to shift his primary attention from the problems of art to those of society when the following chapters relate art to the lack of human hope that Ruskin believes to be a consequence of the Reformation. According to him, after the Reformation when men first lost their firm belief in an afterlife, they could not attain peace of mind or die hopefully, and he discusses four pairs of major artists to show the effect of belief or its lack upon their art – Salvator and Dürer, Claude and Poussin, Wouverman and Fra Angelico, and Giorgione and Turner. After Ruskin has shown the environment in which Turner's mind took form, he devotes a chapter each to detailed interpretation of two works that represent the faith of the artist and his England. These paintings, *Apollo and Python* and *The Garden of the Hesperides*, reveal Turner's fascination with the destruction of beauty and his consequent lack of hope, the cause of which lies in the nature of the age, an age that believes neither in man nor in God and which lets great men die in isolation and despair.

In his next work, *Unto This Last* (1862), which he completed the same year as this final volume of *Modern Painters*, Ruskin turned to attack the economic system that he believed produced such despairing, inhuman relations of men in society. *Unto This Last*, whose four chapters first appeared in 1860 as articles in the *Cornhill*, of which Thackeray was then editor, consolidates the political position Ruskin had been evolving during the previous decade and sets forth the ideas he would continue to advance in *Munera Pulveris* (1862–3), *The Crown of Wild Olive* (1866), *Time and Tide* (1867), and *Fors Clavigera* (1871–84). Most contemporary readers found both Ruskin's general attitudes and his specific proposals so outrageous that they concluded that he must have been struck mad. Today, his political proposals, like his emphases on communal reponsibility, the dignity of labour, and the quality of life, have had such influence that they no longer appear particularly novel. In the beginning of *Unto This Last*, as in *Modern Painters*, Ruskin confronts the so-called experts and denies the relevance of their ideas. Whereas classical economists proceeded on the assumption that men always exist in conditions of scarcity, Ruskin, who realized that a new political economy was demanded by new conditions of production and distribution, argues that his contemporaries in fact exist in conditions of abundance and that therefore the old notions of Malthus, Ricardo, Mill, and others are simply irrelevant. According to him, then, 'the real science of political economy, which has yet to be distinguished from the bastard science, as medicine from witchcraft, and astronomy from astrology, is that which teaches nations to desire and labour for the things that lead to life: and which teaches them to scorn and destroy the things that lead to destruction' (17.85).

In the following pages I propose to look at Ruskin's interpretations of art, society, and his own life. The first kind of interpretation Ruskin undertook focuses on Turner. At first he wished simply to explain Turner's art in the context of the contemporary reviewers' scurrilous attacks and, by taking these reviewers on their own terms, to show his readers how to appreciate the great and insufficiently appreciated artist in their midst. This project quickly clarified itself as a lesson in interpreting perception and then as an exercise in practising the correct, more intense way to see the art and world around one.

Ruskin, who evolved from a clever amateur into a polemical critic and art theorist, from there further developed into a Victorian sage, into, that is, a secular prophet who took all society as his province. Throughout his career he remained polemical and throughout his career he remained equally concerned to make interpretations necessary to his audience's cultural, spiritual, and moral health. These tendentious, polemical interpretations always had a wider purpose, and they almost always included Ruskinian parables of perception that instruct the reader by example how to experience fact and meaning, form and content.

Such a drive to interpret remained a constant in Ruskin's career, despite the many changes that took place as he learned more about art and society, lost his religious faith, and met with adulation and yet incomprehension. One must not, however, overstress the degree of change or the inconsistency in his complex thought, since frequently what is at issue turns out to be more a matter of changed emphasis than an entirely new development. For example, perhaps Ruskin's most obvious and apparently radical shift of interest appears in his evolution from a critic of art to a critic of society. But even this new fervent interest in political economy turns out to be not such a radical departure as it might first appear. Not only did Ruskin never entirely cease writing about art but he also had earlier always been concerned with the effects of art upon its audience. Similarly, when Ruskin shifts increasingly from visual to visionary art, or from aesthetics to iconographical readings of art, these are shifts of emphasis announced in the opening volume of *Modern Painters*, where he states that he will discuss ideas of truth, beauty, and relation in explaining the art of Turner and his contemporaries. Ruskin does at last fulfil his announced plan, but he makes many detours on the way.

Throughout his complex development, however, his urge to educate his contemporaries in the crucial – and crucially related – projects of seeing and understanding their world remains a constant. Ruskinian interpretation, whether of art or society, takes many subjects for its concern. It merges subtly on the one side with seeing, with raw perception, and on the other it blends with definition, the product (and project) of intellectual analysis. As a Victorian sage, Ruskin is first and foremost an exegete, an interpreter and definer of the real, and in the early volumes of *Modern Painters* such a critical project takes various forms. First of all, he sets out to make us *see* –

to see all those beautiful facts of nature which laziness and inadequate artistic conventions have prevented us from perceiving. To enable us to see with his heightened powers, Ruskin relies on his word-paintings, which communicate the experience of his intense encounter with the visual world.

At the same time that Ruskin thus provides his reader with such fables of perception, which interpret raw experience for him, he also formulates a theoretical framework for his contention that art that communicates such heightened experience marks a great advance on the work of the old masters. Here the sage's formulations of the key terms of discourse take the appropriate form of precise explanations of terms basic to the painter's and the critic's art, terms such as 'colour', 'tone', 'beauty', 'imitation', and 'taste'. At the same time, Ruskin, who sets out to explain the superiority of modern landscape painting to that of sixteenth- and seventeenth-century masters, early begins to define and interpret broad movements in art and their relation to broader cultural, political, and religious history. His discussions of the fall of a great culture in *The Stones of Venice*, the rise of landscape art in *Modern Painters III*, and the significance of the picturesque in *Modern Painters IV* exemplify such broader cultural interpretation. As he turns to the criticism of society, this joint concern to define key terms and interpret crucial phenomena remains constant. Therefore, from one point of view all that Ruskin does when he turns a large portion of his attention from art to society is simply to employ many of the same interests in a new area.

In the later works, however, his application of this interpretative bent often has a very different tone largely because the subjects of his interpretation appear more emotionally loaded, more dangerous, as subjects of such discussion. Furthermore, when Ruskin discussed the meaning of Gothic or the true significance of the picturesque, most of his contemporary readers did not find such issues threatening. In his early works, particularly in *Modern Painters* and *The Seven Lamps of Architecture*, he engaged himself to create a larger appreciation, understanding, and audience for painting and architecture, and a large part of his intended audience readily gave itself into Ruskin's hands. To them his assertiveness, rhetorical flourishes, and confessed dislike of the opinion of professional critics only appealed the more. In contrast, when he began to discuss political economy, a project clearly forewarned in the 1853 discussion of 'The Nature of Gothic' in *The Stones of Venice*, Ruskin pointedly confronted his audience and its beliefs. He not only wrote expecting a collision, he wrote increasingly to ensure one. Of course, having taken such an explicitly contentious, hostile approach to his audience's key beliefs about economic and political truths, Ruskin then skilfully deployed a wide range of rhetorical strategies that, in the face of this hostility, could win his audience's forebearance and eventual acceptance. The later applications of his exegetic skill appear in the context of subjects or concerns that are both surprising and even outrageous. Whereas the earlier matters for interpretation, individual paintings, broad cultural movements, or abstract concerns, were the obvious subjects for such an enterprise, the exegetical subjects in the later works take the reader more by surprise.

Such contentiousness, however, does not mark his auto-biography, *Praeterita*, the last of Ruskin's works and the last that we shall examine. Although its gentle, markedly unpolemical tone sets *Praeterita* apart from almost all his other prose, his citations of personal experience remain a constant throughout his long career. His comparisons in the first volume of *Modern Painters* of his experience of La Riccia with Claude's painting of it, his experience of Tintoretto's *Annunciation* in the second, and his similar narration of the experience of landscape in *The Seven Lamps of Architecture* (1849) and of Venice and its surrounds in *The Stones of Venice* (1851–3) are matched by his many relations of personal experience in the works on political economy. 'Traffic', for example, draws upon his encounter with an advertisement in a shop window observed while walking, and his other works present his personal experiences of the contemporary world, occasionally in the form of citations from his letters or diaries. *Praeterita*, too, which grew out of autobiographical chapters in *Fors Clavigera*, his letters to the working men of England, draws upon his characteristic word-painting and dramatization of the experience of meaning to create a new form of self-history. At the end, Ruskin, who had proved such a brilliant interpreter of art and society, proves himself one of the greatest, if most unusual, of autobiographers.

1 Ruskin the word-painter

Throughout his works, Ruskin engages himself to make us see and understand better – two operations that he takes to be intimately and even essentially related. When other writers would use the terms 'think' or 'conceive', he employs visual terminology; and when one expects to encounter the words 'understand', 'grasp', or 'think', he finds, instead, 'see'. Ruskin's theoretical statements, letters, and diaries all make abundantly clear that he assumed many psychological processes generally considered abstract to be visual and to proceed by means of visual images. Such assumptions do much to explain Ruskin's somewhat anachronistic adherence to the theory of visual imagination held by Hobbes, Locke, Addison, and Johnson – a view whose popularity Burke's *On the Sublime* (1757) had greatly undermined in the second half of the eighteenth century. These assumptions also suggest how Ruskin could be so perceptive about the nature and meaning of allegorical images. He believed that most abstractions, in fact, are first formulated mythically or symbolically and that only later does the conscious reason play its part.

Therefore, he believes that all truth is comprehended visually, and to this axiom he joins the corollary that to learn anything one must experience it – see it – for oneself. At the heart of Ruskin's aesthetic theories, practical criticism, and instructions to young artists lies a heartfelt conviction that one can only learn things, one can only know them, by experiencing them for oneself. Such an emphasis might appear particularly paradoxical in the work of a critic like Ruskin so committed, particularly in his later career, to allegorical and symbolical art. But even in regard to such symbolic modes Ruskin, who combines visual and visionary epistemologies, sees no conflict. As he makes clear in his discussions of artistic psychology and symbolic imagery, he believes that both visual and visionary truths are matters of direct experience, for, according to him, they are the way one actually encounters such truths. In other words, he believes that the greatest moral and spiritual truths appear, and have always appeared, to mankind in symbolic form, so that whereas visual truths arise in the exterior world and visionary ones in the interior one of the mind, both are matters of personal experience. According to Ruskin, then, the fact that one only truly learns things, particularly ideas, by experiencing them simultaneously explains the human value of symbolic and visionary art, his own word-painting, and painterly realism.

For Ruskin the chief justification of realism as an artistic style thus resides in its forcing the artist to educate his eye and hand. Such a Ruskinian conception of realism as self-education furnishes the ultimate justification of his famous, if much misunderstood, injunction to young artists to 'go to nature in all singleness of heart, and walk with her laboriously and trustingly, having no other thoughts but how best to penetrate her meaning, and remembering her instruction; rejecting nothing, selecting nothing, and scorning nothing . . . and rejoicing always in the truth' (3.624). Many readers have wondered how Ruskin, who had begun *Modern Painters* to proselytize Turner's late works of haze, swirling rain, and fantastic colours, could have ended his volume with such apparently contradictory instructions to the contemporary artist. Was it that the polemical origins of the work had led him astray? As Ruskin frequently reminds us in the course of this opening volume, he defends Turner's close knowledge of visual fact precisely because the critics of *Blackwood's* and *The Times* had attacked the artist's great works for being 'unlike nature'. The 1844 preface to *Modern Painters I* thus explains: 'For many a year we have heard nothing with respect to the works of Turner but accusations of their want of *truth*. To every observation on their power, sublimity, or beauty, there has been but one reply: They are not like nature. I therefore took my opponents on their own ground, and demonstrated,

by thorough investigation of actual facts, that Turner *is* like
nature, and paints more of nature than any man who ever lived'
(3.51-2). Has Ruskin's understandable desire to show up the
critics who so harshly treated his artistic idol led him so far
from his original intentions that he forgets to defend Turner's
works of the 1840s at all?

As is usually the case with Ruskin, the solution to an
apparent gross inconsistency is readily seen once we look
closely at the context in which it appears. Here Ruskin is most
definitely not urging that all great art must take the form of
realistic transcriptions of visual fact. He is not even addressing
his remarks to mature artists. Rather he addresses the student,
the beginner, emphasizing that 'from young artists nothing
ought to be tolerated but simple *bonâ fide imitation* of nature.
They have no business to ape the execution of masters . . . Their
duty is neither to choose, nor compose, nor imagine, nor
experimentalize; but to be humble and earnest in following the
steps of nature, and tracing the finger of God' (3.623). Even
though Ruskin (and the editors of the Library Edition) caution
that he directs his remarks to beginning students, readers have
frequently misunderstood his point and thought that Ruskin
was here advancing a claim for the artistic superiority of
extreme photographic naturalism as a painterly style. In fact,
immediately after thus instructing the neophyte, Ruskin adds
that when visual experience has nurtured the young artists'
hand, eye, and imagination, 'we will follow them wherever
they choose to lead . . . They are then our masters, and fit to be
so' (3.624). In other words, to paint like Turner, or even to paint
a very different art that could rival his, one first had to begin
with training eye and hand. One, however, cannot stop at this
training stage.

Ruskin made such recommendations because he firmly
believed 'the imagination must be fed constantly by external
nature' (4.288) or, as he put it in somewhat different terms: 'I
call the repesentation of facts the first end; because it is
necessary to the other and must be attained before it. It is the
foundation of all art; like real foundations, it may be little

thought of when a brilliant fabric is raised on it; but it must be there' (3.136–7). Such a conception of artistic development, in which symbolical or even visionary art is seen as growing forth from the visual, explains how Ruskin could have linked his defence of Turner with that of the Pre-Raphaelites, who were then painting shallow, static compositions in a hard-edge realism. His attitude towards the members of the Pre-Raphaelite Brotherhood is summed up in his statements that even though they had not achieved art of the quality of Turner, they were beginners on the right track. He explains in the Addenda to his lecture 'Pre-Raphaelitism' (1854):

> It is true that so long as the Pre-Raphaelites only paint from nature, however carefully selected and grouped, their pictures can never have the character of the highest class of compositions. But, on the other hand, the shallow and conventional arrangements commonly called 'compositions' by the artists of the present day, are infinitely farther from great art than the most patient work of the Pre-Raphaelites. That work is, even in its humblest form, a secure foundation, capable of infinite superstructure; a reality of true value, as far as it reaches, while the common artistic effects and groupings are a vain effort at superstructure without foundation. (12.161–2)

In defending Turner, Ruskin has looked back to his earlier works to reveal that in them the painter had created the necessary foundation that enabled him later to erect a 'brilliant fabric'; in defending the Pre-Raphaelites, a group of young men at the beginning of their careers, he only urged that they had thus far built the necessary foundation.

Ruskin makes personally achieved knowledge of visual fact the foundation of his art theory because he believes that it is only by trying to capture the external world in form and colour that the painter ever learns to apprehend it. Like E. H. Gombrich, he believes that we are more likely to see what we paint than paint what we see. Ruskin emphasizes that because we behold the world by means of conventions, artists have an especially difficult time in seeing the world anew and for themselves since they must break free from both the conventions of everyday seeing and those of artistic representation. According to him, his Victorian contemporaries 'permit, or even compel, their painters and sculptors to work chiefly by rule, altering their models to fit their preconceived notions of what is right'. The sad result of such rules is that 'when such artists look at a face, they do not give it the attention necessary to discern what beauty is already in its peculiar features; but only to see how best it may be altered into something for which they themselves have laid down the laws. Nature never unveils her beauty to such a gaze' (5.99). Furthermore, the effects of such intellectually created rules do not stop with the work of art and the artist who produces it, for the effect is no less 'evil on the mind of the general observer. The lover of ideal beauty, with all his conceptions narrowed by rule, never looks carefully enough upon the features which do not come under his law . . . to discern the inner beauty in them' (5.99). Not only do cultural conventions teach the spectator to judge paintings by a false standard that prevents his enjoyment of novel beauties but they also teach him to perceive, or mis-perceive, the world around him, thus lessening both his pleasure and his knowledge. Ruskin, who here anticipates the work of Gombrich, always insists that art provides the visual vocabularies with which people confront the world around them and by which they experience it. He thus points out, for instance, that 'little as people in general are concerned with art, more of their ideas of sky are derived from pictures than from reality; and that if we could examine the conception formed in the minds of most educated persons when we talk of clouds, it would frequently be found composed of fragments of blue and white reminiscences of the old masters' (3.345–6). For Ruskin, therefore, both artist and audience must learn to perceive with an innocent eye, forgetting what something is supposed to look like and trying to see it without conventional visual vocabularies. Unfortunately, one of the greatest barriers to new knowledge, new experience, of the world is that people see what they think they know to be there rather than what they see before them. As he points out in *A Joy For Ever* (1857), 'one of the worst diseases to which the human creature is liable is its disease of thinking. If it would only just *look* at a thing instead of thinking what it must be like . . . we should all get on far better' (16.126).

Ruskin, one may point out, is one of the few critics and theoreticians in the history of Western art who have granted due importance to the roles of both visual thinking and the physical act of drawing or painting as a means of knowledge. His aesthetic theories here relate importantly to his political views because his recognition of the essential connection that joins the work of eye, hand, and mind in the artistic process leads to his emphasis on the essential dignity of labour. As he argues in *The Stones of Venice*, 'it is only by labour that thought can be made healthy, and only by thought that labour can be made happy, and the two cannot be separated with impunity' (10.201). According to him, contemporary painting, like Renaissance architecture and modern factory work, separated labour from thought and paid a heavy price for doing so.

Ruskin, whose personal experience convinced him that one could only sharpen one's perceptions of the external world by trying to draw it, came as a salutary correction to earlier art theory. In particular, the notion of *ut pictura poesis* – that painting and literature were sister arts possessing many of the same qualities and purposes – had been tried to raise the low status of the visual arts by emphasizing the intellectual nature of the artistic act. Writers, such as Reynolds, who worked with a restricting vocabulary that permitted them to distinguish only between manual and intellectual labour, inevitably gave short shrift to the physical and pre-conscious portions of the artistic process. When Ruskin creates a Romantic version of a sister-arts aesthetic, he replaces the great academician's distinction between intellectual and mechanical art with one that emphasizes a third faculty, the imagination. In this way he can avoid the need to see art as either pure mechanical imitation or intellectualized creation. According to Ruskin, the artist who generalizes by convention fails to make contact with nature and beauty, and as a result his art atrophies. He therefore insists: 'Generalization, *as the word is commonly understood*, is the act of a vulgar, incapable, and unthinking mind. To see in all mountains nothing but similar heaps of earth; in all rocks, nothing but similar concretions of solid matter; in all trees, nothing but similar accumulations of leaves, is no sign of high feeling or extended thought' (3.37; my italics). Ruskin does not, any more than Reynolds, wish art mechanically to transcribe nature, but he emphasizes that the act of generalization – as it is not commonly understood – must be instinctive, unconscious, and imaginative, and it must be prepared for by years of learning to see with one's hand and in one's art.

In *Pre-Raphaelitism* (1851), which argues that all great art derives from the artist's learning to see for himself, Ruskin makes the charge that his contemporaries stifled and corrupted young artists by forcing upon them conventionalized, generalized ideals:

We begin, in all probability, by telling the youth of fifteen or sixteen, that Nature is full of faults, and that he is to improve her; but that Raphael is perfection, and that the more he copies Raphael the better; that after much copying of Raphael, he is to try what he can do himself in a Raphaelesque, but yet original manner: that is to say, he is to try to do something very clever, all out of his own head, but yet this clever something is to be properly subjected to Raphaelesque rules, is to have a principal light occupying one-seventh of its space, and a principal shadow occupying one third of the same; that no two people's heads in the picture are to be turned the same way, and that all the personages represented are to possess ideal beauty of the highest order, which ideal beauty consists partly in a Greek outline of nose, partly in proportions expressible in decimal fractions between the lips and chin; but mostly in that degree of improvement which the youth of sixteen is to bestow upon God's work in general. This I say is the kind of teaching which through various channels, Royal Academy lecturings, press criticisms, public enthusiasm, and not the least by solid weight of gold, we give to our young men. And we wonder we have no painters! (12.353–4)

Ruskin scorns the Neoclassical ideal because, by placing man in a prideful, false relation to nature, it limits instead of enhancing vision. In particular, he believes that such premature reaching after an ideal prevents the young artist from learning to see for himself. And, as Ruskin emphasizes in *Pre-Raphaelitism* (1851), to see for oneself is the foundation of all great art: 'every great man paints what he sees . . . And thus Pre-Raphaelitism and Raphaelitism, and Turnerism, are all one and the same, so far as education can influence them'. Although very different men may employ their abilities to create different kinds of art, they are none the less 'all the same in this, that Raphael himself, so far as he was great, and all who preceded or followed him who ever were great, became so by painting the truths around them as they appeared to each man's mind, not as he had been taught to see them, except by the God who made both him and them' (12.385).

Furthermore, like many Renaissance writers on art, Ruskin believes proportion, design, and artistic composition follow natural laws. But, unlike these earlier art theorists, he does not accept that such laws are reducible to a few central rules or proportions, such as the golden mean. Therefore, Ruskin holds, once again, that the only way the artist can learn either to perceive the beautiful or to compose pictures is by confronting nature in the act of representation. As he explains in *A Joy For Ever* (1857), 'A student who can fix with precision the cardinal points of a bird's wing, extended in any fixed position, and can then draw the curves of its individual plumes without measurable error, has advanced further towards a power of understanding the design of the great masters than he could by reading many volumes of criticism, or passing many months in undisciplined examination of works of art' (16.149). By attempting to capture nature's beauties in a drawing or painting, one sharpens one's perceptions of both nature and art.

Ruskin's attempts to teach his contemporaries how to see do not stop with the theoretical pronouncements he makes throughout his writings. These theories, which provide the foundation for his entire critical enterprise, are intended to defeat the opponents of Turner, to convince his other readers that Ruskin defends him in an obviously rational manner, and to urge young artists, professional and amateur alike, to forge a living relation with the world. Ideally, Ruskin wants every reader to test his ideas by trying to draw the infinite variety of nature himself, and in fact he wrote *The Elements of Drawing* (1857) to promote such a desire. However, realizing that most readers would have to be convinced by his verbal arguments, Ruskin employs his great gift of word-painting to provide his readers with the kind of visual relation to the world he would like them to develop.

Ruskin's word-painting, his characteristic educative and satiric technique in the early works, takes three forms, each more complex than the last. First of all, he employs what we may term an additive style, in which he describes a series of visual details one after another. For example, when describing how effectively Turner paints water in the first volume of *Modern Painters*, he proceeds by dividing his analysis into various visual facts. He thus first points out that Turner correctly represents the energy of a raging ocean by utilizing both the extension as well as the height of the waves. 'All the size and sublimity of nature are given, not by the height, but by the breadth, of her masses; and Turner, by following her in her sweeping lines, while he does not lose the elevation of its surges, adds in a tenfold degree to their power' (3.564). Next, he emphasizes the effect of weight that Turner has managed to create: 'We have not a cutting, springing, elastic line; no jumping or leaping in the waves; *that* is the characteristic of

Chelsea Reach or Hampstead Ponds in a storm. But the surges roll and plunge with such prostration and hurtling of their mass against the shore, that we feel the rocks are shaking under them' (3.564–5).

At this point, having quietly moved from abstract analysis to general description and then to a description of a specific event, he places us within the energies he describes. Immediately afterwards, he adds another 'impression' when he instructs us, 'observe how little, comparatively, they are broken by the wind: above the floating wood, and along the shore, we have indication of a line of torn spray; but it is a mere fringe along the ridge of the surge, no interference with its gigantic body. The wind has no power over its tremendous unity of force and weight' (3.565). Whereas earlier in this passage Ruskin merely mentioned the various visual facts that Turner's art had accurately recorded, he now has subtly moved us into the world of these facts, trying to make his readers see more accurately, see the kind the phenomena they would elsewise have neither confronted nor noticed at all. Ruskin concludes this portion of his description by pointing to yet another fact recorded by Turner's painting, after which he points out its implications. Although this passage has moved from a discussion of abstract qualities to a description of specific embodiments of them, Ruskin has not found it necessary to create a fully imagined space because he follows Turner's work so closely. Although more complex than most other instances of his additive style, this passage characteristically proceeds by adding one set of observed facts to previously mentioned ones.

In contrast, his second form of word-painting proceeds by creating a dramatized scene before us, after which it focuses our attention on a single element that moves through the space he has conjured up with language. For example, when writing about rain clouds, Ruskin explains how they first form and then move in relation to the earth below, and then, like the evangelical preacher and the Romantic poet, he cites his own experience:

I remember once, when in crossing the Tête Noire, I had turned up the valley towards Trient, I noticed a rain-cloud form on the Glacier de Trient. With a west wind, it proceeded towards the Col de Balme, being followed by a prolonged wreath of vapour, always forming exactly at the same spot over the glacier. This long, serpent-like line of cloud went on at a great rate till it reached the valley leading down from the Col de Balme, under the slate rocks of the Croix de Fer. There it turned sharp round, and came down this valley, at right angles to its former progress, and finally directly contrary to it, till it came down within five hundred feet of the village, where it disappeared; the line behind always advancing, and always disappearing at the same spot. This continued for half an hour, the long line describing the curve of a horse-shoe; always coming into existence and always vanishing at exactly the same places; traversing the space between with enormous swiftness. This cloud, ten miles off, would have looked like a perfectly motionless wreath, in the form of a horse-shoe, hanging over the hills. (3.395)

Ruskin thus sets us before his Alpine scene, permitting us to observe the movement of a single element within it. After he has concluded his examination of the moving cloud, he moves us farther away and tells us what it would look like – how we would experience it – from a different vantage point.

In such a passage of description Ruskin proceeds by placing us before a scene, making us spectators of an event. By permitting (or forcing) the reader to see with his eyes, he simultaneously achieves several goals: first, he furnishes us with a standard by which works of art purporting to convey natural fact can be tested; second, by permitting us access to his perceptions – by permitting us to see with his eyes – he allows (or forces) us to perceive specific natural facts we may never have noticed or understood before; third, by so doing, he makes one of his major points, namely, that the external world contains innumerable beautiful phenomena most people never perceive or even realize exist; finally, by making this demonstration on his own pulses, as it were, Ruskin demonstrates to the reader his dependence upon him, for without Ruskin few readers would encounter these phenomena.

In Ruskin's third and most elaborate form of word-painting, he develops his role of Master of Experience even more fully. Now he sets us within the depicted scene itself, makes us participate in its energies, and here fulfils his own descriptions of imaginative art. Several passages in *Modern Painters* explain that both the novice and the painter without imagination must content themselves with a topographical art of visual fact. 'The aim of the great inventive landscape painter', on the other hand, 'must be to give the far higher and deeper truth of mental vision, rather than that of the physical facts, and to reach a representation which . . . shall yet be capable of producing on the far-away beholder's mind precisely the impression which the reality would have produced' (6.35). As the opening volume explains, in this higher form of art 'the artist not only *places* the spectator, but . . . makes him a sharer in his own strong feelings and quick thoughts' (3.134). The great imaginative artist, in other words, grants us the privilege of momentarily seeing with his eyes and imaginative vision; we experience his phenomenological relation to the world.

Ruskin achieves this goal in language by employing what we may anachronistically term a cinematic prose; that is, he first places himself and his reader firmly in position, after which he generates a complete landscape by moving his centre of perception, or 'camera eye', in one of two ways. He may move us progressively deeper into the landscape in a manner that anticipates cinematic use of the zoom lens, or he may move us laterally across the scene while remaining at a fixed distance from the subject – a technique that similarly anticipates the cinematic technique called panning. By thus first establishing his centre of observation and then directing its attention with patterned movement, Ruskin manages to do what is almost impossible – create a coherent visual space with language.

Such a procedure, which he employs when describing both works of art and the natural world they depict, appears, for instance, in his brilliant description of La Riccia in the first volume of *Modern Painters* and in many crucial passages in *The Stones of Venice*, including his magnificent tour of Saint Mark's, his aerial view of the Mediterranean Sea, and his narration of the approach to Torcello.

This narration of the approach to this (then) desolate island exemplifies a particularly pure form of such cinematic word-painting because Ruskin strives to convey the experience of movement towards this lonely, deserted place. He begins by locating us in space:

> Seven miles to the north of Venice, the banks of sand, which nearer the city *rise* little above low-water mark, *attain* by degrees a higher level, and *knit* themselves at last into fields of salt morass, raised here and there into shapeless mounds, and intercepted by narrow creeks of sea. One of the feeblest of these inlets, after *winding* for some time among buried fragments of masonry, and knots of sunburnt weeds whitened with webs of fucus, *stays* itself in an utterly stagnant pool beside a plot of greener grass covered with ground ivy and violets. (10.17; my italics)

As my italicization of several words in this passage reveals, Ruskin infuses even this quiet, desolate scene with energy by here relying on active verbs and generally avoiding passives. These verbs provide a movement that leads the eye into the scene even as it creates it, and having created before the reader's eye the island of Torcello, Ruskin then selfconsciously places himself and his reader in that scene:

> On this mound is built a rude brick campanile, of the commonest Lombardic type, which if we ascend towards evening (and there are none to hinder us, the door of its ruinous staircase swinging idly on its hinges), we may command from it one of the most notable scenes in this

wide world of ours. Far as the eye can reach, a waste of wild sea moor, of a lurid ashen grey; not like our northern moors with their jet-black pools and purple heath, but lifeless, the colour of sackcloth, with the corrupted sea-water soaking through the roots of its acrid weeds, and gleaming hither and thither through its snaky channels. No gathering of fantastic mists, nor coursing of clouds across it; but melancholy clearness of space in the warm sunset, oppressive, reaching to the horizon of its level gloom (10.17)

Having approached this desolate island and then climbed its abandoned bell tower with Ruskin, we find our gaze directed successively in each of the directions of the compass, after which he instructs us to look down at Torcello itself and notice the four small stone buildings, one of them a church, which 'lie like a little company of ships becalmed on a far-away sea' (10.18). After describing the buildings and the distant view of Venice more fully, he then guides our emotional reaction to what we have seen when he remarks that 'the first strong impression which the spectator receives from the whole scene is, that whatever sin it may have been which has on this spot been visited with so utter a desolation, it could not at least have been ambition' (10.20).

Ruskin's perhaps surprising introduction of the notion that only punishment for sin could have produced such desolation reminds the reader that he has taken us to Torcello, as he has taken us to Venice itself, to explain in the manner of an Old Testament prophet how to read a warning for England in the fate of an earlier commercial and military power. Ruskin characteristically finds such warnings in the evidence of Venetian architecture and its relation to the workers who created it, for he argues that the movement from Gothic to Renaissance styles embodies Venetian secularization and a consequent turning away from the pious Christianity which, he believes, orginally founded its strength. Therefore, when he takes us to Torcello, the first island on which the eventual founders of Venice settled in their flight from the mainland, he wishes both to contrast it in its present desolation with its daughter, Venice, and to emphasize how Torcello's founders, who took literally the notion that the church was their ark of salvation, had a faith tragically long since lost. Therefore the remainder of the chapter concerns itself with examining the cathedral on the island and what it meant to its original builders. But to create this effect, Ruskin first skilfully employs his cinematic style to move us through the Venetian lagoon so that we experience the approach to this desolate place with some of the same feelings as the original settlers, who had fled mainland wars.

Such effective passages are thus hardly mere embellishments of his main argument, nor are they self-indulgent displays of virtuosity – though in his early works, particularly the first volume of *Modern Painters*, Ruskin certainly enjoyed such virtuosity. His word-painting is not even a tactic that he employs to smooth over the rough spots in an argument. Such writing in fact is central to Ruskin's conception of himself as critic and sage. Since he relies upon this cinematic prose to educate his audience's vision, teaching its members to see shapes, tone, colours, and visible fact they have often confronted but failed to observe, these descriptions are basic to his conception of himself as one who teaches others to see, experience, and understand. Such writing also serves to establish what the older rhetoricians called the speaker's *ethos*. The main problem for the Victorian sage is to convince others that he is worth listening to, that he is a man whose arguments – however strange they may at first appear – are the products of a sincere, honest, and above all reliable, mind. One of the first tasks of any speaker or writer is to establish himself before his audience as a believable, even authoritative, voice; and this Ruskin easily accomplishes by demonstrating that he has seen and has seen more than the critics who oppose him. His critics are blind, and he has vision.

These passages of highly wrought prose take their place as part of a larger structure of argument. They serve, in fact, as a major part of that complex rhythm of satire and Romantic vision which characterizes the proceedings of the Victorian sage. In the earlier volumes of *Modern Painters*, where Ruskin employs it to defend Turner against the claims of older art, this rhythm takes the form of a satirical word-painting of a work by an old master followed by Ruskin's description of either a similar work by Turner or a scene the older work was supposed to represent. For example, in his chapter 'Of the Truth of Colour' in the first volume of *Modern Painters*, he first looks at Gaspar Poussin's *La Riccia* in the National Gallery, after which he presents his own impressions of the original scene. Writing with heavy sarcasm, Ruskin easily conveys the impression that the painting so prized by the critics who treated Turner's advanced work cruelly does not concern itself with presenting the facts of a particular place:

> It is a town on a hill, wooded with two-and-thirty bushes, of very uniform size, and possessing about the same number of leaves each. These bushes are all painted in with one dull opaque brown, becoming very slightly greenish towards the lights, and discover in one place a bit of rock, which of course would in nature have been cool and grey beside the lustrous hues of foliage, and which, therefore, being moreover completely in shade, is consistently and scientifically painted of a very clear, pretty, and positive brick red, the only thing like colour in the picture. The foreground is a piece of road which, in order to make allowance for its greater nearness, for its being completely in light, and, it may be presumed, for the quantity of vegetation usually present on carriage roads, is given in a very cool green grey; and the truth of the picture is completed by a number of dots in the sky on the right, with a stalk to them of a sober and similar brown. (3.277–8)

Immediately after presenting this harshly sarcastic rendering of the painting attributed to Gaspar Poussin, Ruskin employs his familiar strategy of citing his own experience of a scene ineptly presented in a work of visual art:

Not long ago, I was slowly descending this very bit of carriage-road, the first turn after you leave Albano . . . It had been wild weather when I left Rome, and all across the Campagna the clouds were sweeping in sulphurous blue, with a clap of thunder or two, and breaking gleams of sun along the Claudian aqueduct lighting up the infinity of its arches like the bridge of chaos. But as I climbed the long slope of the Alban Mount, the storm swept finally to the north, and the noble outline of the domes of Albano, and the graceful darkness of its ilex grove, rose against pure streaks of alternate blue and amber; the upper sky gradually flushing through the last fragments of rain-cloud in deep palpitating azure, half aether and half dew. The noonday sun came slanting down the rocky slopes of La Riccia, and their masses of entangled and tall foliage, whose autumnal tints were mixed with the wet verdure of a thousand evergreens, were penetrated with it as with rain. I cannot call it colour, it was conflagration. Purple, and crimson, and scarlet, like the curtains of God's tabernacle, the rejoicing trees sank into the valley in showers of light, every separate leaf quivering with buoyant and burning life; each, as it turned to reflect or to transmit the sunbeam, first a torch and then an emerald. Far up into the recesses of the valley, the green vistas arched like the hollows of mighty waves of some crystalline sea, with the arbutus flowers dashed along their flanks for foam, and silver flakes of orange spray tossed into the air around them, breaking over the grey walls of rock into a thousand separate stars, fading and kindling alternately as the weak wind lifted and let them fall. Every glade of grass burned like the golden floor of heaven, opening in sudden gleams as the foliage broke and closed above it, as sheet-lightning opens in a cloud at sunset. (3.278–9)

In setting forth his satiric examination of *La Riccia*, Ruskin quickly dismisses the original work because he wishes to concentrate only on the element of colour, a point on which he finds it particularly easy to praise Turner and to attack his predecessors.

Here as elsewhere, Ruskin convinces us of his position by means of a superbly controlled alternation of vision and satire, preparing us for his polemic at each step of the way by allowing us to borrow his ideas and see. His skill at presenting us with his experience of landscape and landscape art continually makes us feel that his critical opponents and the painters he attacks both work from theory, from recipes, rather than from vision.

2   Ruskin the interpreter of the arts

When Ruskin devoted entire chapters in his fifth volume (1860) to detailed interpretations of individual paintings by Turner, he sounded a note that had been well prepared for from his earliest writing. As his autobiography shows, he learned to associate narrative and meaning with pictures at a young age. One of *Praeterita*'s more charming vignettes relates, for example, that each morning while his father shaved, he told his son a story about figures in a water-colour landscape that hung on his bedroom wall.

Margaret Ruskin's teaching her son to read the Scriptures, which provided his knowledge of sacred history and exegetical tradition, had an even more obvious influence on his career as an interpreter of art, for her lesson taught him both basic attitudes towards interpretation and detailed knowledge of traditonal Christian symbolism. Like so many other major Victorian authors; including Carlyle, Newman, Browning, Eliot, Tennyson, Rossetti, and Hopkins, Ruskin learned his interpretative approaches from reading the Scriptures for types and anticipations of Christ. He transferred to interpretations of painting and architecture the evangelical's habit of taking apparently trivial portions of the Bible and from them demonstrating that even there matters of major significance are found. Preachers and authors of Bible commentaries emphasized, for example, that although the rules in the Book of Leviticus for worship in the Temple at Jerusalem might appear completely irrelevant to a modern believer, they contain truths essential for Christians. According to the standard readings, Christians, who realize that the blood of animals cannot absolve guilt, should none the less meditate upon Leviticus both as a prefiguration of Christ and also as a record of man's gradual realization that he needs a saviour. When Ruskin was nine years old, hc took notes on a sermon

39

that made these points, and the various drafts of these sermon records show how completely he understood this interpretative method even as a young boy. In addition, as *The Seven Lamps of Architecture* (1849) reveals, he drew upon this evangelical interpretation of Leviticus when he argued that his contemporaries should build elaborate houses of worship.

Like Ruskin's knowledge of interpretative commonplaces, the fundamental attitudes towards interpretation which he first learned as a young child appear throughout his career. The most important of these basic assumptions is that everything has meaning, that the universe exists as a semiotic entity that one can read if one has the key. In other words, transferring the attitudes and methods of Protestant scriptural interpretation to art, literature, and society, he approaches such secular matters as if they were Holy Scripture.

When Ruskin makes a straightforward typological reading of Tintoretto's Scuola di San Rocco *Annunciation* or of one of Giotto's frescoes in the Arena Chapel, Padua, he simply applies his knowledge of the conventional religious significance of certain images to an art-historical problem. He makes a more extreme, if none the less conventional, application of Victorian Protestant commonplaces when he begins *The Stones of Venice* (1851) with a warning that this city-state provides a type — and warning — of his own nation's fate. A more radical transference occurs, on the other hand, when he bases his notions of mythology in Turner and the Western tradition on interpretative attitudes derived from his childhood Bible reading or when he employs the tripartite pattern of Old Testament prophecy in writing about contemporary society.

Although word-painting dominates the first volume of *Modern Painters*, even its elaborately pictorial set pieces contain elements of interpretation. Already at this early stage in his career, Ruskin believed that confronting a work of art requires that one encounter it both visually and intellectually. For example, as his satirical description of Claude's *Il Mulino* in *Modern Painters I* demonstrates, his satirical attacks often necessarily contained rudimentary iconographical analyses, for when describing what takes place in the picture to his reader, he interprets and comments upon the action depicted.

When Ruskin turns increasingly towards iconological analysis in the second volume, he clearly does not believe he is turning away from experience of a painting by confronting its symbolism. Rather, for Ruskin, one experiences meaning, just as one does light, colour, and form. To provide a full experience of a painting for the reader, therefore, he has to dramatize the process of perceiving both. Such an approach to art appears with particular clarity in his section on the penetrative imagination in the second volume of *Modern Painters*. Describing Tintoretto's *Annunciation* in the Scuola di San Rocco, Venice, Ruskin begins with the spectator's experience of its realism. He starts therefore by pointing out that one first notices the Virgin sitting 'houseless, under the shelter of a palace vestibule ruined and abandoned', surrounded by desolation. The spectator, says Ruskin, 'turns away at first, revolted, from the central object of the picture forced painfully and coarsely forward, a mass of shattered brickwork, with the plaster mildewed away from it'. Such genre details, he suggests, might strike one as little more than a study of the kind of scene the artist 'could but too easily obtain among the ruins of his own Venice, chosen to give a coarse explanation of the calling and the condition of the husband of Mary'. Ruskin, in other words, begins his presentation of this painting by dramatizing the paths the spectator's eye takes as it comprehends first major and then minor visual details. But because he believes that visible form inextricably relates to meaning, he then immediately presents us with an imagined spectator's first conclusions about the meaning of these details: they appear, it seems, to reflect both the painter's contemporary surroundings in a ruined Venice and his modern fascination with the picturesque, that aesthetic mode which delights in ruin.

At this point, Ruskin takes us deeper into the picture's meaning, and he does so by first intensifying our visual experience of it. According to him, if the spectator examines

41

the 'composition of the picture, he will find the whole
symmetry of it depending on a narrow line of light, the edge of
a carpenter's square, which connects these unused tools with
the object at the top of the brickwork, a white stone, four
square, the corner-stone of the old edifice, the base of its
supporting column'. Citing Psalm 118, Ruskin explains that
these details reveal that the entire painting – and all its
coarsely realistic details – bear a typological meaning, for,
according to standard readings of this psalm, it prefigures
Christ. In Tintoretto's *Annunciation*, therefore, the 'ruined
house is the Jewish dispensation: that obscurely arising in the
dawning of the sky is the Christian; but the corner-stone of the
old building remains, though the builder's tools lie idle beside
it, and the stone which the builders refused is become the
Headstone of the Corner' (2.264–5).

Ruskin's guide through Tintoretto's *Annunciation* provides
his reader with a lesson in perception. Using his gifts for word-
painting, iconographical interpretation, and compositional
analysis, Ruskin does not simply tell us what the painting in
question means. Instead, he provides us with a fable or parable
of ideal perception which dramatizes the experience of one who
gradually perceives the meaning of a painting and thus fully
experiences the work of art. Ruskin, who had a gift for
intellectual analysis, understood his role as art critic as
necessarily moving beyond it to an imaginative demonstration
of the experience of meaning. Just as the first volume of *Modern
Painters* teaches his readers how to perceive the worlds of
nature and art, his later ones teach them how to interpret those
worlds, and in both projects, which Ruskin clearly saw
completely intertwined, he concentrates on providing the
reader with models of experience.

Ruskin's analytical description of Tintoretto's *Annunciation* had a major effect upon Victorian art. In particular,
his description of the way commonplace readings of the Bible
could successfully infuse naturalistic detail with an elaborate
symbolism significantly influenced the Pre-Raphaelite
Brotherhood. Students of this movement long thought that

the young William Holman Hunt, John Everett Millais, and Dante Gabriel Rossetti must have been inspired by the first volume of *Modern Painters*, which emphasized that the young student should rely on detailed naturalism to train eye and hand, but Ruskin himself never claimed such influence. Hunt, one of the founding members of the Pre-Raphaelite Brotherhood, related in his memoirs that the critic's second volume came to him as a sublime source of inspiration, precisely because it suggested a means of solving the two major problems that troubled British art – a general weakness of style and technique caused by a reliance on outmoded pictorial convention and the absence of effective pictorial symbolism that could speak to the Victorian audience. Ruskin's presentation of biblical symbolism in his analyses of Tintoretto encouraged the young men both to test artistic convention and to explore the boundaries of painterly realism. By demonstrating how such imagery could infuse the most minute realistic details of a picture with meaning, Ruskin obviously justified including them. Furthermore, his parable of experience, which dramatizes how the spectator gradually realizes the meaning of Tintoretto's painting, also encouraged these young artists to paint a kind of work which demanded that the spectator pay close attention to all such minute details, and thus Ruskin's descriptions encouraged a kind of nineteenth-century emblematic or meditative art. In addition, Ruskin's description of how typology turned an apparently coarse genre subject into high art also provided a solution to what Hunt felt to be one of the chief needs of Victorian painting – the need for a new iconology to replace outmoded allegories and other forms of symbolism that no longer spoke to the age.

   Although Ruskin did not learn of this Pre-Raphaelite debt to his work until after almost three decades had passed, when Hunt thanked him in a letter, he increasingly turned to detailed readings of art after having to defend the Pre-Raphaelites. The need to defend Hunt's paintings, *The Light of the World* (1853) and *The Awakening Conscience* (1853), therefore importantly influenced Ruskin's own career, the student influencing the master, the influenced becoming the influence.

This seeming change of direction in Ruskin's critical enterprise (which none the less was at least partly anticipated by his plan for *Modern Painters*) appears in both *The Stones of Venice* and the volume of *Modern Painters* Ruskin wrote next after sending his famous letters to *The Times* in defence of these young painters. He expanded his notions of artistic symbolism, its relation to the great artist-poet, and its central place in any basic consideration of art. One centre of his new interests appears in his discussions of the entire grotesque mode of imagination, which embodies itself variously in art, architecture, and literature.

Unlike Macaulay, Arnold, and most Victorian critics, Ruskin accepted that allegory and symbolism played an essential role in great art and literature. Indeed, in *Modern Painters III* (1856) he expresses a 'wish that every great allegory which the poets ever invented were powerfully put on canvas, and easily accessible by all men, and that our artists were perpetually exciting themselves to invent more' (5.134). He points out that as far as the authority of the past bears on the question, 'allegorical painting has been the delight of the greatest men and of the wisest multitudes, from the beginning of art, and will be till art expires' (5.134).

Furthermore, while still writing as a believing Christian, he argued that man's love of symbolism, like his instinctive delight in beauty, derives from fundamental laws of human nature that lead man back to the divine. As he explained about the symbolical grotesque in the last volume of *The Stones of Venice* (1853):

> It was not an accidental necessity for the conveyance of truth by pictures instead of words, which led to its universal adoption wherever art was on the advance; but the Divine fear which necessarily follows on the understanding that a thing is other and greater than it seems; and which, it appears probable, has been rendered peculiarly attractive to the human heart, because God would have us understand

that this is true not of invented symbols merely, but of all things amidst which we live; that there is a deeper meaning within them than eye hath seen, or ear hath heard; and that the whole visible creation is a mere perishable symbol of things eternal and true. (11.182–3)

Ruskin, whose evangelical religious heritage continued to colour his thought long after he began to lose his childhood faith, always believed that the mind first perceives difficult truths in symbolic form. Symbolism, both pictorial and literary, thus has a basic, essential epistemological role. Whenever we experience anything too great or too difficult for us to grasp fully – and Ruskin holds that most truths are beyond man – we encounter the grotesque, the term that Ruskin applies to all forms of symbolism.

Ruskin's writings on the grotesque, which stand out as some of the finest critical and theoretical work produced in Victorian England, have two main focuses – theoretical descriptions of the artist, essentially psychological profiles of the kind of mind that creates this artistic mode, and analyses of works of art and literature which embody it. According to *Modern Painters III*, the central form or mode of the grotesque arises from the fact that the imagination 'in its mocking or playful moods . . . is apt to jest, sometimes bitterly, with under-current of sternest pathos, sometimes waywardly, sometimes slightly and wickedly, with death and sin; hence an enormous mass of grotesque art, some most noble and useful, as Holbein's Dance of Death, and Albert Dürer's Knight and Death, going down gradually through various conditions of less and less seriousness in an art whose only end is that of mere excitement, or amusement by terror' (5.131). In addition to this darker form of the grotesque, which includes work ranging from traditional religious images of death and the devil to satire and horrific art, there is a comparatively rare form that arises 'from an entirely healthful and open play of the imagination, as in Shakespere's Ariel and Titania, and in Scott's White Lady' (5.131). This delicate fairy art is so seldom achieved because 'the moment we begin to contemplate sinless beauty we are apt to get serious; and moral fairy tales, and other such innocent work, are hardly ever truly, that is to say, naturally, imaginative; but for the most part laborious inductions and compositions. The moment any real vitality enters them, they are nearly sure to become satirical, or slightly gloomy, and so connect themselves with the evil-enjoying branch' (5.131–2). In other words, human beings have a natural tendency to discover (or impose) meaning in the facts they encounter.

The third form of the grotesque, which served as the basis for Ruskin's conception of a high art suited to the Victorian age, is the 'thoroughly noble one . . . which arises out of the use or fancy of tangible signs to set forth an otherwise less expressible truth; including nearly the whole range of symbolical and allegorical art and poetry' (5.132). Ruskin, who valuably perceived that fantastic art and literature form part of a continuum that includes sublime, symbolic, grotesque, and satirical work, makes the individual image the centre of his discussion. As he next explains, 'A fine grotesque is the expression, in a moment, by a series of symbols thrown together in a bold and fearless connection, of truths which it would have taken a long time to express in any verbal way, and of which the connection is left for the beholder to work out for himself; the gaps, left or overleaped by the haste of the imagination, forming the grotesque character' (5.132). Drawing upon Spenser's description of envy in the first book of *The Faerie Queene*, he points out that the poet

> desires to tell us, (1) that envy is the most untamable and unappeasable of the passions, not to be soothed by any kindness; (2) that with continual labour it invents evil thoughts out of its own heart; (3) that even in this, its power of doing harm is partly hindered by the decaying and corrupting nature of the evil it lives in; (4) that it looks every way, and that whatever it sees is altered and discoloured by its own nature; (5) which discolouring, however, is to it a veil, or disgraceful dress, in the sight of others; (6) and that

it never is free from the most bitter suffering, (7) which cramps all its acts and movements, enfolding and crushing it while it torments. All this has required a somewhat long and languid sentence for me to say in unsymbolical terms, – not, by the way, that they *are* unsymbolical altogether, for I have been forced, whether I would or not, to use *some* figurative words; but even with this help the sentence is long and tiresome, and does not with any vigour represent the truth. (5.132)

Spenser, on the other hand, puts all of these ideas 'into a grotesque, and it is done shortly and at once, so that we feel it fully, and see it, and never forget it' (5.133). To demonstrate the power, concision, and sheer memorability of such symbolic statement, Ruskin then quotes the poet's emblematic portrait of envy, to which he attaches numbers referring to his own preliminary interpretation:

>   'And next to him malicious Envy rode
> (1)   Upon a ravenous wolfe, and (2, 3) still did chaw
>   Between his cankred teeth a venemous tode,
>   That all the poison ran about his jaw.
> (4, 5) All in a kirtle of discoloured say
>   He clothed was, y-paynted full of eies;
> (6)   And in his bosome secretly there lay
>   An hateful snake, the which his taile uptyes
> (7)   In many folds, and mortall sting implyes'. (5.133)

Ruskin concludes that Spenser has compressed all this material in nine lines, 'or, rather in one image, which will hardly occupy any room at all on the mind's shelves, but can be lifted out, whole, whenever we want it. All noble grotesques are concentrations of this kind, and the noblest convey truths which nothing else could convey' (5.133). Furthermore, the minor examples of this symbolic mode convey truth with a delight 'which no mere utterance of the symbolised truth would have possessed, but which belongs to the effort of the mind to unweave the riddle, or to the sense it has of there being an infinite power and meaning in the thing seen, beyond all that is apparent' (5.133).

Ruskin's analysis of Tintoretto's *Annunciation* in the second volume of *Modern Painters*, Spenser's Ate from *The Faerie Queene* in the third, Turner's *Garden of the Hesperides* and *Apollo and Python* in the fifth, and Milton's 'Lycidas' in *Sesame and Lilies* all exemplify this kind of sophisticated interpretative analysis so rare in nineteenth-century criticism.

In the fifth volume of *Modern Painters* (1860), the simple, straightforward interpretation, which characterized his reading of Spenser, is replaced by putting the object of interpretation against the background – or within the context – of a collection of works, all of which together constitute a tradition. During the fourteen years that passed between the writing of the second and the fifth volumes of *Modern Painters* major changes took place in the religious faith that had originally founded Ruskin's interpretative methods. Ruskin, who wrote *Modern Painters II* as a fervent evangelical, drew heavily upon his religious heritage in it for argument, authority, and rhetoric, just as he did in *The Seven Lamps of Architecture* (1849). By the time he came to write *The Stones of Venice* (1851–3), his faith, while still relatively firm, had become more tolerant, and for the first time he even defended Roman Catholicism to his predominantly Protestant audience. By 1856, when he wrote the next two volumes of *Modern Painters*, his faith had gradually weakened under the blows of geology and contemporary approaches to the Bible; and although he still drew upon his religious heritage for evidence and method, he no longer made the Scriptures the centre of any argument. After his decisive loss of belief in 1858, Ruskin spent several decades wavering between agnosticism and outright, if unannounced, atheism. *Modern Painters V* (1860), the first major work written after his abandonment of Christianity in Turin, makes no explicit statement of his changed religious allegiance, but the new attitudes towards man, art, and society which appear reveal that a radical development has taken place. Ruskin's earlier praise of asceticism and Purist Idealism has been replaced by scorn for those who do not emphasize the primacy of life in this world, and his earlier theological emphases have been replaced by something like a concern for a religion of humanity. Since Ruskin's loss of belief effectively removed the basis of his earlier defences of beauty and art, he found yet another reason for stressing the capacity of art to convey truth. However, just as he found additional reasons for teaching his readers how to interpret art, the original basis of his interpretative methods vanished, too. Fortunately, he easily replaced it by concentrating on the value of myth and other forms of tradition.

According to Ruskin, myth is a special form of the symbolical grotesque which veils 'a theory of the universe under the grotesque of a fairy tale' (12.297). Ruskin, who increasingly became attracted to the study of myth when he lost his faith in the Bible as a divinely inspired text, applies to myth interpretative techniques learned in Bible study. He can thus apply these procedures because he still accepts that moral and spiritual truths reside in traditional texts. After he abandons his Protestant faith, however, he no longer takes any one text as divinely ordained, for as he comes increasingly to place his emphasis on human beings rather than upon a divine father, he also places more importance upon received wisdom. No longer accepting any single privileged text, Ruskin thus willingly perceives that of many different ones each contains some portion of necessary truth, and thus finding truth in so many different places, he, like so many moderns, tries to constitute a tradition by assembling its major texts.

Continuing a practice he had begun long before, Ruskin applies habits of mind and methods of reading first learned in Bible study to the interpretation of these texts, including pagan myths. For instance, like the Bible, a myth indicates the presence of meanings by an enigmatic literal or narrative level. As he explains in *The Queen of the Air* (1869), 'A myth, in its simplest definition, is a story with a meaning attached to it, other than it seems to have at first; and the fact that it has such a meaning is generally marked by some of its circumstances being extraordinary, or, in the common use of the word, unnatural' (19.296). Ruskin further explains that if he informed the reader 'Hercules killed a water-serpent in the lake of Lerna, and if I mean, and you understand, nothing more than that fact, the story, whether true or false, is not a myth' (19.296). If, however, he intends this story of Hercules' triumph to signify that he purified many streams, the tale, however simple, is a true myth. Since audiences will not pay enough attention to such simple narratives, Ruskin, or any creator of myth, must 'surprise your attention by adding some singular circumstance . . . And in proportion to the fulness of intended meaning I shall probably multiply and refine upon these improbabilities' (19.296). In other words, Ruskin applies to myth the points he made about the symbolical grotesque thirteen years earlier. Myth, like Spenserian allegory, communicates 'truths that nothing else could convey' (5.133) with a combination of awe and delight that derives from the mind's effort to solve enigmas, 'or to the sense it has of there being an infinite power and meaning in the thing seen, beyond all that is apparent' (5.133). Furthermore, after Ruskin loses his evangelical religion, he not only considers mythology, like the Bible, a source of spiritual and moral truth, he also interprets it, like the Bible, in terms of multiple meanings.

Ruskin most elaborately applies his conceptions of myth as communally created symbolical grotesques to art criticism in the fifth volume of *Modern Painters* (1860). He begins his reading of Turner's *Garden of the Hesperides* by first explaining the significance of the Hesperid nymphs and the dragon who guards the edenic garden, after which he comments upon the Goddess of Discord and the dark, gloomy atmosphere of the picture, and he explains, 'The fable of the Hesperides had, it seems to me, in the Greek mind two distinct meanings; the first referring to natural phenomena, and the second to moral' (7.392). Quoting at length from Smith's *Dictionary of Greek and Roman Geography*, he concludes that nymphs of the west, or Hesperides, are . . . natural types, the representatives of the soft western winds and sunshine, which were in this district most favourable to vegetation. In this sense they are called daughters of Atlas and Hesperis, the western winds being cooled by the snow of Atlas. The dragon, on the contrary, is the representative of the Sahara wind, or Simoom, which blew over the garden from above the hills on the south, and forbade all advance of cultivation beyond their ridge. But, both in the Greek mind and in Turner's, this natural meaning of the legend was a completely subordinate one. The moral significance of it lay far deeper. (7.392–3)

Explaining that in this second sense the Hesperides are connected not 'with the winds of the west, but with its splendour' (7.393), he draws upon Hesiod to demonstrate that they represent those moral forces and attitudes that reproduce 'household peace and plenty' (7.396). According to him, the names of the individual myths embody moral meanings: 'Their names are, Aeglé, – Brightness; Erytheia, – Blushing; Hestia, – the (spirit of the) Hearth; Arethusa, – the Ministering' (7.395). He then explains that these four were appropriate guardians of the golden fruit that earth gave to Juno at her marriage:

Not fruit only: fruit on the tree, given by the earth, the great mother, to Juno (female power), at her marriage with Jupiter, or *ruling* manly power (distinguished from the tried and *agonizing* strength of Hercules). I call Juno, briefly, female power. She is, especially, the goddess presiding over marriage, regarding the woman as the mistress of a household. Vesta (the goddess of the hearth), with Ceres, and Venus, are variously dominant over marriage, as the fulfilment of love; but Juno is pre-eminently the housewives' goddess. She therefore represents, in her character, whatever good or evil may result from female ambition, or desire of power: and, as to a housewife, the earth presents its golden fruit to her, which she gives to two

51

kinds of guardians. The wealth of the earth, as the source of household peace and plenty, is watched by the singing nymphs – the Hesperides. But, as the source of household sorrow and desolation, it is watched by the Dragon. (7.395–6)

This dragon, to whom Ruskin devotes the largest part of his reading, embodies covetousness and the fraud, rage, gloom, melancholy, cunning, and destructiveness associated with it. Turner, as a great artist, takes his place with the ancient creators of myth, for he too acccepts the meanings of the past and then recasts them in new ways. For the great English painter thus to add new significance to old myth, he had to have had an imaginative insight into their meaning, and in the course of explicating *The Garden of the Hesperides* Ruskin remarks: 'How far he had really found out for himself the collateral bearings of the Hesperid tradition I know not; but that he had got the main clue of it, and knew who the Dragon was, there can be no doubt', since his conception of the dragon 'fits every one of the circumstances of the Greek traditions' (7.401–2). This convergence of ancient and modern arises partly in the fact that Turner perceived the 'natural myth' at the heart of his subject and partly in his knowledge of the Greek tradition. Reading this painting, Ruskin draws upon Homer, Hesiod, Euripides, Virgil, Dante, Spenser, Milton, and the Bible.

Turning to the Goddess of Discord, Ruskin finds that she symbolizes 'the disturber of households' (7.404), though in fact she is the same power as Homer's spirit of the discord of war. 'I cannot get at the root of her name, Eris', Ruskin admits. 'It seems to me as if it ought to have one in common with Erinnys (Fury); but it means always contention, emulation, or competition, either in mind or words'. The final task of Eris, Ruskin concludes, is essentially that of division, and he cites Homer and Virgil to show that the tradition conceives of her as 'always double-minded; shouts two ways at once (in *Iliad*, xi. 6), and wears a mantle rent in half (*Aeneid*, viii. 702). Homer

52

makes her loud-voiced, and insatiably covetous' (7.404).
Turner combines the conception of discord found in classical
literature with Spenser's Ate from *The Faerie Queene* and adds
'one final touch of his own. The nymph who brings the apples
to the goddess, offers her one in each hand; and Eris, of the
divided mind, cannot choose' (7.405–6). As Ruskin explains
the significance of this figure in the painting, he does not
proceed as would one with undoubted authority or one who has
access to a privileged, unitary text. Instead, he admits his lack
of certainty about certain interpretations, points out
potentially contrary readings, and proposes various solutions.
The reader sees him groping with the images in Turner's work
as they turn out to reveal more and more complex meanings.
In other words, Ruskin is again dramatizing the process of
interpretation, for we watch him piecing together the meaning
of this rich, complex, completely relevant work.

After he has demonstrated how he arrives at meanings of
each of the main figures in the painting, Ruskin concludes:

> Such then is our English painter's first great religious
> picture; and exponent of our English faith. A sad-coloured
> work, not executed in Angelico's white and gold; nor in
> Perugino's crimson and azure; but in a sulphurous hue, as
> relating to a paradise of smoke. That power, it appears, in
> the hill-top, is our British Madonna: whom, reverently, the
> English devotional painter must paint . . . Our Madonna –
> or our Jupiter on Olympus – or, perhaps, more accurately
> still, our unknown God. (7.407–8)

In brief, Turner's darkened, dragon-watched garden sets forth
in visible form the spiritual condition of England. It testifies
that England, having exchanged faith in God for faith in gold,
turns away from the path of life, embracing that of death, and
longs to enter an earthly paradise that will be, not Eden, the
garden of God, but the garden of Mammon in which the head
of the serpent, unbruised by Christ, gazes about in icy triumph.
Ruskin calls this a religious picture because it expounds the

faith by which his contemporaries live and work, the faith, that is, to which their deeds, though not their words, testify.

Ruskin's interpretative *tour de force* in setting forth the meaning of *The Garden of the Hesperides* demonstrates with peculiar clarity how completely entwined criticism of art and society had become by the time he wrote the last volume of *Modern Painters*. In the following chapter we shall observe the way he applied many of the same interpretative methods to read the signs of his own times as he had to both earlier and contemporary arts.

3   Ruskin the interpreter of society

Ruskin's chapter on Turner's *The Garden of the Hesperides*, which displays his interpretations of an individual painting at their most complex, shows that for him any work of art always leads to the society within which it took form. His means of moving from art to society in his analysis of this painting exemplify both his characteristic manner of proceeding as a social critic and his most important ideas about society. Immediately after explaining its mythological or symbolic figures, he offers an interpretation of the entire work which concludes that Turner's representation of ancient Greek myth is in fact a nineteenth-century 'religious picture' because it expounds the faith by which his contemporaries live and work, the faith, that is, to which their deeds, if not their words, testify. 'Here, in England, is our great spiritual fact for ever interpreted to us – the Assumption of the Dragon' (7.408). Turner, the greatest of British painters, looks about him, observes the triumph of Mammon, and firmly, if sadly, sets down in the guise of a symbolical grotesque the truth he has observed.

According to Ruskin, Turner darkens his palette to 'a sulphurous hue, as relating to a paradise of smoke' (7.407–8) to show that by choosing to live beneath the watchful glance of the Dragon of Mammon, England entered the true Dark Ages. In the third volume of *Modern Painters* (1856), Ruskin had earlier argued that 'the title ''Dark Ages'', given to the mediaeval centuries, is, respecting art, wholly inapplicable. They were, on the contrary, the bright ages; ours are the dark ones . . . We build brown brick walls, and wear brown coats . . . There is, however, also some cause for the change in our own tempers. On the whole, these are much *sadder* ages than the early ones; not sadder in a noble and deep way, but in a dim wearied way – the way of ennui, and jaded intellect, and uncomfortableness of soul and body' (5.321). When he comes to interpret Turner's *Garden of the Hesperides*, Ruskin concludes that the ennui, the sadness, the lack of light and colour arise, as he believed Turner to have stated, in the worship of what he later termed the Goddess of Getting-on. In taking Turner's *Garden of the Hesperides* as a sign of the times, an index to the spiritual condition of contemporary England, Ruskin sounds a note he will sound with increasing frequency throughout his career as a critic of society.

Ruskin opens the major phase of his career as a social critic, then, by interpreting Turner's painting just as he had opened his career as an art critic by defending its accuracy. Essentially, he proceeds by transforming individual works, as he had earlier transformed individual Venetian buildings, into symbolical grotesques; or, to put it another way, he reads paintings and buildings alike for the meanings they embody. At an early stage of his career – in fact, by the first volume of *The Stones of Venice* (1851) – some of the meanings that compel his attention are social, political, and economic, and by 1860 he applies approaches first used when explaining art to contemporary society.

Throughout his writings on political economy Ruskin depends on a series of aggressive interpretations, and they play a central role in his presentation of himself as a Victorian sage. What makes him a secular prophet in the manner of Carlyle, however, is not his act of interpretation but the fact that he chooses to interpret matters that his audience rarely realizes require interpretation at all. Who, for example, would have expected Turner's *Garden of the Hesperides* to contain such a message for Victorian society, and, similarly, who except a sage would realize that the development of architectural styles in Venice or an industrial accident in England could contain truth essential for England's survival? Indeed, what makes Ruskin, Carlyle, and others like Thoreau or Arnold sages is precisely that they venture to read – interpret – apparently trivial matters such as the colour of contemporary men's clothing, advertisements, and the like, which most members of the audience consider without interest and value. Such is the sage's claim to authority, however, that he can demonstrate that virtually any contemporary phenomenon or incident offers him a direct way into matters of supreme importance – matters such as the cultural health of a nation, its moral nature, and its treatment of the working, producing classes.

This same urge to draw his contemporaries' attention to apparently trivial phenomena that turn out to contain important political and moral truths also informs some of Ruskin's most seemingly quixotic public projects, such as the utopian St. George's Guild and the repair of Hinksey Road, Oxford, by a crew of Oxford undergraduates. Like his interpreting apparently trivial matters, these activities were intended in large part to be exemplary and educational. They were intended to show, for example, the dignity of labour, the necessity of community, and the possibility of non-competitive social organization. Such public gestures were bound to appear quixotic because they forced upon the attention of his contemporaries Ruskin's unfashionable, subversive political economy. Just as his interpretations of perception and symbols have the dual purpose of winning the reader's assent both to the specific interpretation and to the procedure that produces that reading, so, too, these more expansive interpretations have two purposes. First, Ruskin wants to convince us of his interpretations of British society, and second, he wishes us to learn how to make such interpretations ourselves.

Therefore, when he later explains the development of his political views in *Praeterita*, he characteristically presents their evolution in terms of learning to interpret. A visit to the Domecqs, his father's business associates, amid their Parisian elegance presented him with an enigma that demanded interpretation. As a young boy, he wondered why the Andalusians who grew the grapes for the Pedro Domecq sherries 'should virtually get no good of their own beautiful country but the bunch of grapes or stalk of garlic they frugally dined on; that its precious wine was not for them, still less the money it was sold for' (35.409). Later Ruskin felt himself troubled even more because these gentle, generous people 'spoke of their Spanish labourers and French tenantry, with no idea whatever respecting them but that, except as producers by their labour of money to be spent in Paris, they were cumberers of the ground' (35.409). These attitudes, says Ruskin, 'gave me the first clue to the real sources of wrong in the social laws of modern Europe; and led me necessarily into the political work which has been the most earnest of my life' (35.409). When Ruskin explains the development of his political interpretations, he presents himself as an outsider and an onlooker, and he suggests that even as a child he found himself asking questions about matters whose obviousness and urgency the adults around him failed to notice.

Following the procedure that informed the previous two chapters, this one will first summarize some of Ruskin's central ideas and then examine those characteristically Ruskinian techniques he developed to present them. First, let us look at the essential emphases of his social criticism. Like his conceptions of the arts, his ideas about political and social economics combine the traditional and the radically new, the expected and the outrageous. As a disciple of Thomas Carlyle, he forces contemporary England to recognize precisely what its actions and ideologies imply. In particular, he makes the individual members of his audience perceive that their basic attitudes towards work, value, wealth and social responsibility contradict the Christian religion that supposedly forms and informs their lives. This part of the Ruskinian enterprise is crucial because, as contemporary observers of the Victorian scene from Engels to the Christian Socialists pointed out, the moneyed classes so effectively segregated the lives of the lower classes – so effectively kept them out of *sight* – that they did not know the sufferings of the industrial, urban poor.

One fundamenal portion of Ruskin's task, then, is to thrust such facts into sight and consciousness, thereby creating that awareness which is a necessary precondition of moral and social reform. In 'Traffic' (1865) Ruskin thus mocks his audience's conception of an ideal life by presenting it in the form of what is essentially a dream-vision. Arguing that his listeners' worship of the Goddess of Getting-on implies that they also condemn others to miserable lives, he presents a picture of their ideal that enforces corollaries or implicit points they would willingly leave out of their sight and consciousness.

> Your ideal of human life then is, I think, that it should be passed in a pleasant undulating world, with iron and coal everywhere under it. On each pleasant bank of this world is to be a beautiful mansion, with two wings; and stables, and coach-houses; a moderately-sized park; a large garden and hot-houses; and pleasant carriage drives through the shrubberies. In this mansion are to live the favoured votaries of the Goddess; the English gentleman, with his gracious wife, and his beautiful family; he always able to have the boudoir and the jewels for the wife, and the beautiful ball dresses for the daughters, and hunters for the sons, and a shooting in the Highlands for himself. At the bottom of the bank, is to be the mill; not less than a quarter of a mile long, with one steam engine at each end, and two in the middle, and a chimney three hundred feet high. In this mill are to be in constant employment from eight hundred to a thousand workers, who never drink, never strike, always go to church on Sunday, and always express themselves in respectful language. (18.453)

As Ruskin points out, this image of human existence might appear 'very pretty indeed, seen from above; not at all so pretty, seen from below' (18.453), since for every family to whom the Englishman's deity is the Goddess of Getting-on, one thousand find her the 'Goddess of *not* Getting-on' (18.453). By making explicit the implications of such a vision of life based upon an ideal of competition, Ruskin's symbolical grotesque serves a powerful satiric purpose. His rich experience and expertise as an art critic here turns out to be particularly helpful, for he carefully explains the sketched-in elements of his supposedly ideal scene with the same techniques that he uses in his descriptions of an Alpine landscape, the city of Venice, or Turner's paintings. In each case he proceeds by presenting visual details and then drawing attention to their meaning. Here he first presents a slightly tongue-in-cheek image of the English capitalist's Earthly Paradise, after which he reveals its dark implications by showing the world of have-nots upon which this kind of paradise rests. By moving through his created word picture from upper to lower, he endows each portion of his visual image with a moral and political value: the upper classes reside literally, spatially, above the industries that provide their wealth and also above the workers who slave to make their lives ones of ease.

As this typical example of Ruskin's polemic makes clear, he applies the stylistic, interpretative, and satiric techniques which characterized his art criticism to his writings on society. Of course, the fundamental reason he can move so easily from writing about Turner and Tintoretto to writing about the labour question and definitions of value, wealth, price, and production lies in the fact that the same attitudes towards co-operation and hierarchy inform both his areas of concern – areas of concern which Ruskin finds inevitably and inextricably interrelated. For example, when defining composition in the fifth volume of *Modern Painters*, he emphasizes that aesthetic rules and relationships are subcategories of more universal laws of existence. 'Composition may best be defined as the help of everything in the picture by everything else' (7.205), or, again, it 'signifies an arrangement, in which everything in the work is thus consistent with all things else, and helpful to all else' (7.208-9), and the artist is therefore a person who 'puts things together, not as a watchmaker steel', but who puts life into them by arranging his materials 'so as to have in it at last the harmony or helpfulness of life' (7.215). The arts and the work of the artist are therefore images of fundamental laws of life and society, for 'the highest and first law of the universe – and the other name of life is, therefore, "help." The other name of death is ''separation.'' Government and co-operation are in all things and eternally the laws of life. Anarchy and competition, eternally, and in all things, the laws of death' (7.207). Here we have the centre of Ruskin's social, political, and economic thought: a vision of hierarchical and paternalist (or familial) forms of co-operative social organization, a vision which Paul Sawyer astutely sees as essentially Confucian.

As Ruskin's application of the same techniques and ideas to the criticism of art and society reminds us, he does not shift abruptly from writing about painting to writing about political economy. In fact, as early as the chapter on 'The Nature of Gothic' in *The Stones of Venice* (1853), he had indicted modern society for alienating and dehumanizing its workers by forcing them to perform mechanical, soul-destroying tasks, and in his 1854 pamphlet *On the Opening of the Crystal Palace*, which associated oppressing the poor with the destruction of the past and its beauties, he savagely juxtaposed the self-indulgence of a dinner party to the starving of the poor. In his Manchester lectures published under the title of *The Political Economy of Art* (1857) and later reissued as *A Joy For Ever* (1880), Ruskin introduces his distinction between true and false wealth and argued that a love of true wealth implied a wish to eradicate poverty and unemployment. Attacking advocates of classical *laissez-faire* economics in their own stronghold, Manchester, he instructed its millowners and merchants that 'the notion of Discipline and Interference lies at the very root of all human progress or power' and that the ' ''Let-alone'' principle is . . . the principle of death' (16.26). At this point in his career as a social economist, Ruskin believed that those with political and economic power simply failed to perceive their true responsibilities.

By 1860, when he wrote the individual essays that constitute *Unto This Last* (1862), on the other hand, he had become convinced that they would never perceive these responsibilities until they first realized that their fundamental socio-economic assumptions were pseudo-scientific justifications of selfishness and shortsightedness. The first section of

Unto This Last, which argues that one cannot formulate a useful economic theory without paying attention to the social affections, therefore attacks the intellectual status of *laissez-faire* economics, particularly in its popularized forms, and the third, which concerns economic justice, attacks its fundamental immorality. The remaining sections advance his own complex humanized conceptions of value, price, production, consumption, and wealth. According to Ruskin, 'THERE IS NO WEALTH BUT LIFE. Life, including all its powers of love, of joy, of admiration' (17.105), and therefore the measure of a thing's value is the extent to which it aids life and the living.

Ruskin's social criticism eventually had major influence in part because he thus rejected outright the fundamental ideas of classical economics accepted by most of his contemporaries and set out on his own. Drawing upon the Bible, Carlyle, Owen, and the example of the Middle Ages, Ruskin's Tory Radicalism thus opposed Malthusian emphases upon scarcity of resources and instead stressed their abundance and a consequent need for just and efficient distribution. Similarly, he rejected a political economy based upon competition and urged the greater relevance and practicality of one based on co-operation. Working from premises that thus differ radically from those of his contemporaries, Ruskin in *Unto This Last* redefines 'wealth' and transfers emphasis from production to consumption, thus advancing a consumerist ethic:

> Economists usually speak as if there were no good in consumption absolute. So far from this being so, consumption absolute is the end, crown, and perfection of production; and wise consumption is far more difficult than wise production. Twenty people can gain money for one who can use it . . . The final object of political economy, therefore, is to get good method of consumption, and a great quantity of consumption: in other words, to use everything, and to use it nobly; whether it be substance, service, or service perfecting substance. (17.98, 102)

His assumptions about the nature of wealth and consumption lead him to urge that 'Production does not consist in things laboriously made, but in things serviceably consumable; and the question for the nation is not how much labour it employs, but how much life it produces. For as consumption is the end and aim of production, so life is the end and aim of consumption' (17.104).

In addition to these general attitudes that horrified many of his contemporaries, Ruskin advanced specific political programmes that they found equally radical and equally disturbing. He urged, for example, that the government should establish 'training schools for youth' and that 'every child born in the country should, at the parent's wish, be permitted (and, in certain cases, be under penalty required) to pass through them' (17.21). He also proposed that the government not only should take care of all old and indigent but also should establish factories to employ those in need of work. These factories, which would set standards of quality for British manufacturing by example, would also ensure that people on all economic levels could obtain pure, unadulterated food and other necessities.

Of all Ruskin's proposals, however, few struck many contemporaries as more outrageous than the one exhorting them to disregard Malthusian doctrine and pay workers a living wage. To the economists who stated that raising wages would lead the worker either to overproduce his class or to drink himself to death, Ruskin replies: 'Suppose it were your own son of whom you spoke, declaring to me that you dared not take him into your firm, nor even give him his just labourer's wages, because if you did he would die of drunkenness, and leave half a score of children to the parish. ''Who gave your son these dispositions?'' – I should enquire. Has he them by inheritance or by education?' (17.106). And it is the same, he insists, with the poor. Ruskin, later a proponent of a classless society, points out that either members of the lower classes have essentially the same nature as the rich and hence are capable of education or they 'are of a race essentially different from ours, and unredeemable (which, however often implied, I have heard none yet openly say)' (17.106). Ruskin, who applied his skill at biblical and pictorial interpretation to the language of political economy, was particularly astute at finding the claims of self and class interest lurking within supposedly objective explanations.

Indeed, Ruskin particularly embarrassed and outraged many readers – just as he inspired others, such as Morris and Gandhi – when he pointed out that the cruellest treatment of the poor by the rich appears not in poor wages and working conditions but in the way they are kept down by mental and spiritual impoverishment. 'Alas! it is not meat of which the refusal is cruellest, or to which the claim is validest. The life is more than the meat. The rich not only refuse food to the poor; they refuse wisdom; they refuse virtue; they refuse salvation' (17.106–7). In *Time and Tide* (1867) and *Fors Clavigera* (1871–8, 1880–4) he continues to advance a series of specific proposals based upon his hierarchical, co-operative, familial social vision – namely, that all should work and all do some physical labour, that wages should be fixed by custom, as he believed they were in the professions, and not set by any law of supply and demand; that the nation and not individuals should own natural resources; and that government should take responsibility for education, which he took to be that factor most productive of true wealth.

Like his Tory Radicalism itself, the language in which Ruskin presents his criticism of contemporary society combines old and new, for in attacking crude *laissez-faire* capitalism and its associated social attitudes, he draws upon the rhetoric, vocabulary, and tone of both Old Testament prophecy and Victorian preaching. From the beginning Ruskin had a tendency to preach. When he was but three years old, he gathered the family servants around him, climbed on a chair, and urged them, 'People, be good!' The same urge to preach – and the same basic message – colours all his writings. He necessarily exchanges the techniques of the preacher, one whose congregation accepts him as superior, for those of the alienated secular prophet who self-consciously sets himself apart from his audience when he comes to criticize his society. Ruskin changes his conception of himself as a writer only when he advances essentially unpopular ideas. None the less, whether writing more as preacher or as prophet, Ruskin applies the exegetical methods learned in Bible study.

Of course, when the preacher interpreted even apparently trivial passages, he still dealt with the Bible, a sacred text. Ruskin, in contrast, makes his elaborate interpretations of contemporary phenomena and so emulates the prophets of the Old Testament more than he does contemporary preachers. In so doing, he also follows Carlyle, who developed a variety of strategies to convince an unwilling listener, for the sage writes (or speaks) not only as an interpreter but also as one whose interpretations will be received with hostility. His first task, therefore, must be to win the attention of his audience and then to convince its members that he is worthy of their credence. Ruskin, like Carlyle and other Victorians who wrote in this mode, employs a variety of methods to win his reader's attention and eventual allegiance. The rest of this chapter will examine the literary techniques and rhetorical strategies that characterize his social, economic, and political writings, and as we shall observe, many of Ruskin's techniques as a sage relate so essentially to his ideas that form and content are not easily separated. The examples of Ruskinian technique adduced in the following pages therefore also permit us to examine the major points in his social criticism.

All Ruskin's techniques derive from his need to convince an audience many of whose basic ideas he is attacking. For example, Ruskin makes extensive use of the related techniques of definition, redefinition, and satirical definition to demonstrate that, however little his readers might suspect the fact, they do not know the correct meaning of words. Their words have lost meaning, which must be restored if these words are to exist in any sort of healthy, correct relation to reality. One may compare Ruskin's definitions in *Modern*

Painters with those in his later social criticism. When writing of art, Ruskin defines a host of concepts – imitation, truth (in the visual arts), composition, beauty, sublimity, picturesqueness, tone, colour, form, and grand style. Such definitions provide the usual material of art treatises, of course, and Ruskin's reader expects him to make them. But when he undertakes more radical and far more disturbing definitions of value, wealth, and religion in his later works, Ruskin thrusts the act of definition into the foreground, thereby demonstrating his audience's complete dependence upon him since only he can provide the true meaning of words crucial to whatever discussion he has embarked upon. For example, *Unto This Last* combines its definitions of key terms with scathing attacks on more conventional ones. According to Ruskin,

> Political economy (the economy of the State, of citizens) consists simply in the production, preservation, and distribution, at fittest time and place, of useful or pleasurable things . . . But mercantile economy, the economy of 'merces' or of 'pay', signifies the accumulation in the hands of individuals, or legal and moral claim upon, or power over, the labour of others; every such claim implying precisely as much poverty or debt on one side, as it implies riches or right on the other. (17.44–5)

Believing that the most basic definitions of classical economists are incorrect because they misconceive their entire subject, he further attacks one economist's definition of his subject as ' "the science of getting rich". But there are many sciences, as there are many arts, of getting rich. Poisoning people of large estates, was one employed largely in the Middle Ages; adulteration of food of people of small estates, is one employed largely now' (17.61). In essence, Ruskin claims by these manœuvres that since his audience has fallen away from the ways of God (or nature), its members find themselves hobbled by a corrupted, misleading, almost useless language and they need him to restore their words. They need him, in other words, to lead them forth from the Tower of Babel. His emphasis upon definition exemplifies the way Ruskinian theme and technique coalesce and become almost indistinguishable, for he believes that the false moral, economic, and political positions that he opposes not only cause unhappiness and obvious societal problems but even have corrupted the language we all use.

As Ruskin's use of definition suggests, his pronouncements frequently take the form of an alternation of satire and vision – satire to destroy opposing ideas and moments of vision to replace them. In addition to redefining the ideas and language of his opponents satirically, Ruskin also employs other forms of satire. Many of his acts of interpretation themselves take the form of satiric sallies, for as he probes his society's ideas and values, the demeaning conclusions he draws again and again demonstrate that its members have fallen away from their supposed standards of morality and humanity.

By performing elaborate acts of interpretation upon trivial phenomena, which he claims to be windows into a nation's heart, he essentially metamorphoses such matters into elaborate satirical allegories or symbolical grotesques. Ruskin frequently employs two kinds of this formal device, which we may in turn call 'found' and 'invented' versions of the symbolical grotesque. Found or discovered satiric grotesques are those he locates in existing phenomena. For instance, his discussion of wealth and value in *Unto This Last* (1860) includes a newspaper report of a shipwrecked man who strapped all his gold to himself in an attempt to preserve it, leapt from the sinking vesel, and promptly plunged to the bottom of the sea. Ruskin, who engages himself to examine modern notions of value and ownership, asks the question, Now does the man own the gold or does the gold own the man? In contrast to such discovered satirical grotesques, invented ones, which take the shape of both individual images and parables, do not have a component furnished by contemporary phenomena. These satiric images and parables are exemplified by his image of England's true divinity, Britannia of the Market, in 'Traffic' (1865) or, in the same work, his fable of the two supposedly friendly landowners who spend all their funds on weapons to defend themselves against each other.

These forms of the grotesque contribute to the sage's dominant technique, which is the creation of *ethos* or credibility. According to the older rhetoricians, arguments may take three forms or modes: *logos*, *pathos*, or *ethos*. Arguments that depend upon *logos* employ what we may loosely term 'reason', for they attempt to convince by means of logic, authority, statistics, precedent, testimony, and such like, whereas those that employ *pathos* appeal to the emotions of the listener or reader. In contrast, *ethos* tries to convince the audience that the speaker or writer is a serious, sincere, and, above all, trustworthy person, one whom, when the resolution of an argument lies hanging in the balance, one should follow. Of course, virtually any kind of argumentation draws variously upon all three argumentative modes. But Ruskin proceeds by making all his various arguments and evidence convince the audience that, however much his ideas might seem strange and even outrageous, he deserves their credence. Because he begins from an ideological position that conflicts with that of his audience, he starts with a decided disadvantage; and forced to take grave rhetorical risks, he does so to demonstrate how unusually, how unexpectedly he turns out to be right while received, orthodox opinion turns out to be wrong. All of Ruskin's other techniques – his clear argumentation, his citation of personal experience, his word-painting, his clear sight, and his ability to notice natural phenomena most fail to observe – contribute to creating this appearance of credibility, so that we will pay attention to his most annoying or unexpected ideas, give them some consideration, and allow him the opportunity to convince us both that they are true and that our recognition that they are true is crucial to us personally.

In contrast to 'found' symbolical grotesques which the sage creates from those phenomena he chooses to interpret, the invented form of the symbolical grotesque derives from his own imagination and may take the forms of extended analogies, metaphors, and parables. In his writings on political economy Ruskin makes great use of such invented symbolical grotesques, which there effectively replace the word-painting that characterized his art criticism as his favourite rhetorical device. In 'The Roots of Honour', which opens *Unto This Last*, he uses precisely such a satirical analogy to attack the intellectual stature of nineteenth-century economic theory. Thus, he begins with a corrective introduction that first attacks as delusions these supposedly scientific approaches to society's major problems and then compares them to primitive, outmoded bodies of thought, such as alchemy: 'Among the delusions which at different periods have possessed themselves of the minds of large masses of the human race, perhaps the most curious – certainly the least creditable – is the modern *soi-disant* science of political economy, based on the idea that an advantageous code of social action may be determined irrespectively of the influence of social affection' (17.25). Granting that 'as in the instances of alchemy, astrology, witchcraft, and other such popular creeds, political economy has a plausible idea at the root of it' (17.25), Ruskin argues that the economists err disastrously by 'considering the human being merely as a covetous machine' (17.25). Although he readily agrees that one should attempt to eliminate inconstant variables when trying to determine guiding laws for any area of knowledge, he points out that economists have failed to perceive that 'the disturbing elements' in the problem they have tried to eliminate from their theories are not the same as the constant elements since 'they alter the essence of the creature under examination the moment they are added; they operate, not mathematically, but chemically, introducing conditions which render all our previous knowledge unavailable' (17.26). Drawing upon his knowledge of chemistry, a true science, for an analogy, Ruskin then points out how dangerous such false conclusions can be: 'We made learned experiments upon pure nitrogen, and have convinced ourselves that it is a very manageable gas: but, behold! the thing which we have practically to deal with is its chloride; and this, the moment we touch it on our established principles, sends us and our apparatus through the ceiling' (17.26). Immediately after introducing his satiric analogy, which takes the form of a rudimentary, abbreviated narrative, Ruskin next employs a wonderfully bizarre symbolical grotesque:

Observe, I neither impugn nor doubt the conclusion of the science if its terms are accepted. I am simply uninterested in them, as I should be in those of a science of gymnastics which assumed that men had no skeletons. It might be shown, on that supposition, that it would be advantageous to roll the students up into pellets, flatten them into cakes, or stretch them into cables; and that when these results were effected, the re-insertion of the skeleton would be attended with various inconveniences to their constitution. The reasoning might be admirable, the conclusions true, and the science deficient only in applicability. Modern political economy stands on a precisely similar basis. (17.26)

According to Ruskin, who is arguing that this supposedly practical science is in fact decidedly impractical and impracticable, modern political economy had the same advantages and disadvantages as does his invented pseudo-science of gymnastics-without-skeletons: its inventors and practitioners have sacrificed usefulness, relevance, and applicability to theoretical elegance and ease. In making such a charge, Ruskin immediately demonstrates that although he might at first appear the wild-eyed impractical theorist, his ideas have more value than commonly accepted ones.

Ruskin's invented symbolical grotesques are particularly useful in summing up the flaws in opposing positions. These analogies and little satiric narratives of course owe much to Neoclassical satirists, particularly Swift, whose *Tale of a Tub* and *Gulliver's Travels* make extensive use of both to cast an opposing view in a poor light. When Ruskin argues in 'Traffic' against those who claim that they cannot afford to create beautiful surroundings for human life, he employs a characteristic parable to reduce such protests to absurdity. Suppose, he instructs his listeners, that he had been sent for 'by some private gentleman, living in a suburban house, with his garden separated only by a fruit wall from his next door neighbour's' (18.438) to advise him how to furnish his drawing-room. Finding the walls bare, Ruskin suggests rich furnishings, say, fresco-painted ceilings, elegant wallpaper, and damask curtains, and his client complains of the expense, which he cannot afford. Pointing out that his client is supposed to be a wealthy man, he is told:

> 'Ah yes,' says my friend, 'but do you know, at present I am obliged to spend it nearly all on steel-traps?' 'Steel-traps! for whom?' 'Why, for that fellow on the other side of the wall, you know: We're very good friends, capital friends; but we are obliged to keep our traps set on both sides of the wall; we could not possibly keep on friendly terms without them, and our spring guns. The worst of it is, we are both clever fellows enough; and there's never a day passes that we don't find out a new trap, or a new gun-barrel, or something.' (18.438–9)

Fifteen million a year, his client tells Ruskin, the two good neighbours spend on such traps, and he doesn't see how they could do with less and so Ruskin the room decorator must understand why he has so little available capital to beautify his client's environment. Turning to his audience, Ruskin abandons the pose of the naïf and comments in the tones of the Old Testament prophet: 'A highly comic state of life for two private gentlemen! but for two nations, it seems to me, not wholly comic.' Bedlam might be comic, he supposes, if it had only one madman, and Christmas pantomines are comic with one clown, 'but when the whole world turns clown, and paints itself red with its own heart's blood instead of vermilion, it is something else than comic, I think' (18.439). Having first mocked with his satiric parable the intellectual seriousness of his listeners' self-justifications for failing to spend money on beautifying their environments, Ruskin next moves from mocking to damning them as he reveals, once again, that competition is a law of death and that it destroys art, beauty, and the conditions of healthy, full existence.

In the manner of the Old Testament prophet he demonstrates that the actions of his contemporaries reveal that they have abandoned the ways of God. Ruskin's symbolical grotesques provide a particularly appropriate device for such social criticism, because they emphasize both the symbolical and the grotesque qualities in contemporary life which desperately need correction. These set pieces, which combine Ruskin's gifts for interpretative and satirical virtuosity, replace word-painting as his characteristic stylistic technique in the later writing and prove essential to his enterprise as a sage, for they serve to focus his interpretations of society while providing an attractive, interesting, and often witty means of conveying his ideas.

4   Ruskin interpreting Ruskin

Ruskin, the great master of interpreting art and society, brings his skills to bear on his own life in *Praeterita*, the incomplete autobiography he published in separate numbers between 1881 and 1886, after which year recurrent attacks of madness forced him to stop writing. He wrote *Praeterita* for many reasons. It was, he tells us, 'an old man's recreation in gathering visionary flowers in fields of youth', and it was also a 'dutiful offering at the grave' (35.11–12) of his parents. He wrote it chiefly, however, as a means of enabling us to see how he learned or developed his main ideas. According to Ruskin, 'How I learned the things I taught is the major, and properly, the only question regarded in this history', and such a statement of purpose makes two important points. First, unlike Rousseau, Ruskin does not conceive his autobiography as a complete self-revelation or confession. It does not therefore include any mention of his ill-fated marriage or, for that matter, of many of his friendships, and neither does it discuss large portions of his career. Attacks of madness that forced him to give up writing before he had covered certain subjects, rather than conscious avoidance of them, explains many, though not all, of these major omissions.

Ruskin's statement of purpose also informs us that *Praeterita*, like Mill's autobiography, records largely an intellectual history, and so it does in a peculiarly Ruskinian sense – in the sense that arises in his dual emphases upon the visual sources of knowledge and upon the intrinsic unity of human sensibility. For Ruskin, no such being as economic, aesthetic, or intellectual man exists – even for the sake of argument. According to him, there exists only the human being, all of whose experiences are interconnected, entwined, relevant.

But for Ruskin all his own experiences centre upon acts of perception, and he therefore presents his life history as a series of juxtaposed moments of vision. Ruskin's autobiography thus weaves together his two concerns with perception and interpretation, and although he occasionally emphasizes either learning to see or learning to understand in individual episodes, he more commonly interweaves the history of both parts of his education because he finds them so essentially related.

Interpretation explicitly enters the tale of his life when he relates the importance of his childhood reading of the Bible: 'It had never entered into my head to doubt a word of the Bible, though I saw well enough already that its words were to be understood otherwise than I had been taught; but the more I believed it, the less it did me any good' (35.189). He soon learned that even the Bible, which evangelicals took as the literal word of God, could not simply be read. It demanded interpretation.

By the mid-1850s Ruskin found his childhood evangelical belief, which provided the core of his interpretations of art and life, increasingly threatened by geology, the Higher Criticism, and his own doubts. These various pressures soon led, he tells us, to 'the inevitable discovery of the falseness of the religious doctrines in which I had been educated' (35.482). *Praeterita* borrows but recasts the narrative of his decisive break with evangelicalism which had appeared in the April 1877 issue of *Fors Clavigera*. *Fors* tells that the 'crisis' in his thought came one Sunday morning in Turin 'when, from before Paul Veronese's Queen of Sheba, and under quite overwhelmed sense of his God-given power', he went to the Protestant chapel only to hear the preacher there assure his Waldensian congregation that they, and only they, would escape the damnation that awaited all others in the city. 'I came out of the chapel, in sum of twenty years of thought, a conclusively *un*-converted man' (29.89). According to this earlier version, then, the pastor's statements about damnation, which so contradicted Ruskin's own sense of the ways of God, finally enabled him to choose between 'Protestantism or nothing' (29.89). In contrast, *Praeterita* states that he *first* attended the Waldensian sermon and then encountered the painting by

Veronese. Furthermore, according to this second version of his past, Ruskin did not react strongly against the sermon or break sharply with his evangelical belief before he left the chapel. Instead, feeling the sermon irrelevant rather than infuriating, he walked out of the chapel unmoved, and only later did the music and painting convince him that there were better ways than the evangelical to serve God.

When Ruskin inverted the order of events, placing the sermon before his experience in the gallery, he changed the point of his narrative; for whereas *Fors* explains how a painting convinced him that his evangelical religion preached a false doctrine of damnation, *Praeterita* tells how the arts of painting and music taught him how to serve God better than his earlier belief. *Praterita* not only fails to mention the crucial fact that his decision was between 'Protestantism or nothing', thereby lessening the sense of crisis, but also emphasizes affirmation rather than denial.

The contradictions that appear when one compares Ruskin's two versions of this turning point in his life reveal how much interpretation dominates the autobiographer's task. The evidence of Ruskin's letters and diaries suggests that the earlier, harsher version of the incident in *Fors* more accurately describes what took place on that balmy afternoon in Turin, but once he returned to some form of Christian belief in 1875, he naturally began to perceive unifying rather than disrupting elements in his past experience.

Ruskin thus organizes his past life chiefly in terms of moments of vision because he conceives himself essentially as a spectator, as one, that is, who lives chiefly by seeing and is fully alive only when engaged in the act of vision. *Praeterita* presents this view of himself by concentrating upon the development of his sense of sight, and the crucial facts in his development stand out as moments when he first saw or learned to see in some new, important way. He lays no claim to artistic imagination, intelligence, or 'any special power or capacity; for, indeed, none such existed, except that patience in looking, and precision in feeling, which afterwards, with due industry, formed my analytic power . . . On the other hand', he tells us, 'I have never known one whose thirst for visible fact was at once so eager and so methodic' (35.51). His auto-biography, which therefore takes the form of showing the ways he developed under the influence of this 'thirst for visible fact', points out that satisfying this thirst provided one of the young Ruskin's chief sources of childhood delight. As a young child, he had few toys and chiefly amused himself by exploring patterns in the carpets and fabrics in his home.

Such a life of the eye was also encouraged by the way in which the Ruskins made their European tours, neither speaking the language of the countries they visited nor socializing with other British tourists. According to him, such removal has its own benefits, for 'if you have sympathy, the aspect of humanity is more true to the depths of it than its words; and even in my own land, the things in which I have been least deceived are those which I have learned as their Spectator' (35.119). *Praeterita*, then, is an autobiography of Ruskin the Spectator, the man who sees and understands.

The Spectator, *Praeterita* makes poignantly clear, is also one who stands apart from the flow of life and looks on. *Praeterita*, which relates that his parents' social insecurities largely deprived him of friends his own age, emphasizes his 'perky, contented, conceited, Cock-Robinson-Crusoe sort of life' and his family's social isolation – what Ruskin calls 'our regular and sweetly selfish manner of living'. Thus isolated, he concerned himself largely with the visual and the visionary – studying things close at hand or imagining those far away: 'Under these circumstances, what powers of imagination I possessed, either fastened themselves on inanimate things – the sky, the leaves, and pebbles, observable within the walls of Eden – or caught at any opportunity of flight into regions of romance' (35.37). Ruskin thus came to love the life of one who sees others without himself being seen: '*My* times of happiness had always been when *nobody* was thinking of me . . . My entire delight was in observing without being myself noticed – if I could have been invisible, all the better'

(35.165–6). According to Ruskin, his childhood love of thus being an almost invisible, seeing eye produced his 'essential love of *Nature*' which was the 'root of all that I have usefully become, and the light of all I have rightly learned' (35.166). This love, his autobiography tells us, was nurtured by his childhood surroundings, which he continually characterizes in terms of a lost Garden of Eden to which he no longer has access except perhaps in memory.

In addition to characterizing Ruskin's sense of sight and explaining how it developed, *Praeterita* also documents the education of his eye by relating his various encounters with drawing teachers, specific landscapes, and works of art. It explains, for example, that although his drawing-master, Charles Runciman, did nothing to encourage his gift for 'drawing delicately with the pen point', he none the less taught the young Ruskin 'perspective, at once accurately and simply' and 'a swiftness and facility of hand which I found afterwards extremely useful, though what I have just called the "force", the strong accuracy of my line, was lost' (35.76–7). Most important, Runciman 'cultivated in me – indeed founded – the habit of looking for the essential points in things drawn, so as to abstract them decisively, and explained to me the meaning and importance of composition' (35.77).

Ruskin's autobiography also explains that encounters with specific works of art or artistic sites directly influenced his life and career. Sometimes such encounters took place under the guidance of a more experienced eye, such as occurred at a gathering at the home of Samuel Rogers, the banker-poet. Ruskin relates that when he 'was getting talkative' in praise of a Rubens sketch that his host owned, the artist George Richmond asked why he hadn't commented upon the much greater Veronese hanging beneath it. To Ruskin's surprised response that the Venetian seemed quite tame in comparison with the Rubens, Richmond answered that, nevertheless, 'the Veronese is true, the other violently conventional' (35.337). Comparing Veronese's clear shadows with Rubens's use of ochre, vermilion, and asphalt outline, he thus led the young art critic to a new understanding of Venetian colour and the nature of artistic convention.

Most of the encounters Ruskin describes, in contrast, took place without the assistance of others and were purely individual discoveries. For example, when visiting Genoa in 1840 Ruskin saw 'for the first time the circular Pietà by Michael Angelo, which was my initiation in all Italian art. For at this time I understood no jot of Italian painting, but only Rubens, Vandyke, and Velasquez' (35.264), and, similarly, his 1845 visit to Lucca first taught him that architecture was more than an excuse for the picturesque. Ruskin, who had a Romantic love of picturesque time-worn structures, suddenly encountered twelfth-century buildings built 'in material so incorruptible, that after six hundred years of sunshine and rain, a lancet could not now be put between their joints' (35.350). As a young man he had learned, like all romantically inclined, artistically sensitive people of the time, to seek out the pleasing irregularities and age mark of the picturesque, and for a time he patterned his own drawing style after that of Samuel Prout, who invented a particular kind of urban picturesque. Lucca taught him, however, that great architecture was more than merely an excuse for picturesque seeing. In fact, it had its own rules of form which the seeker of the picturesque inevitably failed to perceive. The picturesque, for all its delights, therefore turned out to be another one of those artistic conventions that ultimately did more harm than good because it masked, rather than aided, seeing what was really there. Having approached this beautiful medieval town to enjoy the delicate pleasures of the picturesque, Ruskin unexpectedly found anti-picturesque buildings, for instead of succumbing to the effects of time, these Gothic structures still retained their strength, firmness, and precise outline.

Venice, one of the centres of his life and thought, also at first appeared to him largely as a stimulus for Romantic imaginings. Like so many eighteenth- and nineteenth-century travellers, he easily fell under its spell. Ruskin, whose autobiography takes form around moments of perception, characteristically describes his love of Venice originating in a single sight, although one less obviously exciting or epiphanic than those he describes occurring in the Alps: 'The beginning of everything was in seeing the gondola-beak come actually inside the door at Danieli's, when the tide was up, and the water two feet deep at the foot of the stairs; and then, all along the canal sides, actual marble walls rising out of the salt sea, with hosts of little brown crabs on them, and Titians inside' (35.295). Having approached Venice through Byron and Turner, Ruskin immediately fastened the nuances of their art to his own perceptions. According to him, the great moment of revelation about Venice came, not when he encountered the palaces along the Grand Canal or the Ducal Palace, or even Saint Mark's, but when he first saw Tintoretto's great cycle of paintings on the life of Christ. At the urging of his friend and drawing-master J. D. Harding, he visited the Scuola di San Rocco, where his encounter with Tintoretto's masterful cycle forced him, he says, to study the culture and history of Venice, and thus he came to write *The Stones of Venice*.

The most important discoveries Ruskin reports in *Praeterita* appear in several skilfully narrated parables of perception that explain how he learned to see for himself. His presentation of the famous incidents of the Norwood ivy and the Fontainebleau aspen reveals that an encounter with Turner's work, specifically his sketches of Switzerland, prepared him for these crucial moments of discovery which, in turn, prepared him to understand Turner even better. Ruskin realized that the sketches of Switzerland, which he so coveted 'were straight impressions of nature – not artificial designs, like the Carthages and Romes. And it began to occur to me that perhaps even in the artifices of Turner there might be more truth than I had understood . . . In these later subjects Nature herself was composing with him' (35.310). Immediately after relating how he came upon this insight into Turner's mode of working, *Praeterita* tells us how Ruskin himself began to see with a cleared vision:

Considering of these matters, one day on the road to Norwood, I noticed a bit of ivy round a thorn stem, which seemed, even to my critical judgement not ill 'composed'; and proceeded to make a light and shade pencil study of it in my grey paper pocket-book, carefully, as if it had been a bit of sculpture, liking it more and more as I drew. When it was done, I saw that I had virtually lost all my time since I was twelve years old, because no one had told me to draw what was really there! (35.311)

Ruskin purposively contrasts 'critical judgement' and the act of drawing, sculpture and ivy round a thorn stem, man's art and nature's higher creation. Years of sketching according to the rules followed by the amateur artist in search of the picturesque had left him with a few useful records of place, but not until he forgot himself and casually began to draw this little bit of vegetation did he realize that he had never before 'seen the beauty of anything, not even of a stone – how much less of a leaf!' (35.311)

The next stage in his progress came at Fontainebleau when, weary from walking, he began to draw a little aspen tree and once again experienced a crucial moment of vision after he had almost casually tried to represent a natural fact without paying attention to any rules.

Languidly, but not idly, I began to draw it; and as I drew, the languor passed away: the beautiful lines insisted on being traced – without weariness. More and more beautiful they became, as each rose out of the rest, and took its place in the air. With wonder increasing every instant, I saw that they 'composed' themselves, by finer laws than any known of men. At last, the tree was there, and everything that I had thought before about trees, nowhere! (35.314)

Ruskin remarks that his experience of drawing the Norwood ivy had not 'abased' him so completely because he had always assumed that ivy was an ornamental plant. Drawing a randomly selected tree, however, finally convinced him that nature was greater than art.

> That all the trees of the wood (for I saw surely that my little aspen was only one of their millions) should be beautiful – more than Gothic tracery, more than Greek vase-imagery, more than the daintiest embroiderers of the East could embroider, or the artfullest painters of the West could limn – this was indeed an end to all former thoughts with me, an insight into a new silvan world.
>   Not silvan only. The woods, which I had only looked on as wilderness fulfilled I then saw, in their beauty, the same laws which guided the clouds, divided the light, and balanced the wave. (35.315)

Ruskin believed that his experiences of Turner's Swiss sketches, the Norwood ivy, and the Fontainebleau aspen provided the corner-stone, the foundation, of his future career.

The lessons he learned form the Norwood ivy and the Fontainebleau aspen were continued by his drawing of the Gothic in Rheims. Once again his moment of discovery took him by surprise; for as he drew the tomb of Ilaria de Caretto, he suddenly realized that its beautiful lines followed the same laws that governed the Norwood ivy and the Fontainebleau aspen: The 'harmonies of line . . . I saw in an instant were under the same laws as the river wave, and the aspen branch, and the stars' rising and setting' (35.349). At each stage Ruskin found himself taken by surprise as his eyes and hands taught him to recognize something of crucial importance that his mind did not take in. First, he discovered that the ivy embodies laws of beauty far greater than those inventible by the imagination, and then he found out that trees, which are far more majestic creations of nature, also follow such rules. The third stage in his development arrived when he discovered such laws embodied in the Gothic, a discovery that suggests that the great medieval sculptors and architects had themselves instinctively made this same recognition of the intrinsic beauties of nature which no theorist can encompass or predict.

All of these visual discoveries taught Ruskin the artist that he had to learn to see for himself, and other experiences taught him the same lesson about criticism. Although he occasionally received invaluable guidance, as when Richmond taught him to see Venetian colour, he still had to experience each fact with his own eyes and feelings, and it was for this reason that Ruskin placed such importance upon the act of drawing as a means of the artist's self-education. He traces his independence as a critic to his 1840 visit to Rome when, having been told by parents, friends, and guidebooks what to like in Rome, he quickly discovered that he had to decide about these great buildings and paintings himself: 'Everybody told me to look at the roof of the Sistine chapel, and I liked it; but everybody also told me to look at Raphael's Transfiguration, and Domenichino's St. Jerome' (35.273), which he did not like, and he thus realized he had to make his own judgements.

Like his encounters with the Norwood ivy and the Fontainebleau aspen, *Praeterita's* most powerful epiphanies re-enact occasions when he first encountered some beauty of nature. These more dramatic set pieces present Ruskin seeing something, not close at hand, but far away, for they dramatize prospect visions and Pisgah Sights – moments, that is, when he caught sight of a distant, unattainable paradise. For instance, in 1833, when he was fourteen years old, he arrived in Schaffhausen with his family and at sunset saw the Alps for the first time. Looking out upon a landscape that at first glance resembled 'one of our own distances from Malvern of Worcestershire or Dorking of Kent', he suddenly saw mountains in the distance.

There was no thought in any of us for a moment of their being clouds. They were as clear as crystal, sharp on the pure horizon sky, and already tinged with rose by the sinking sun. Infinitely beyond all that we had ever thought or dreamed – the seen walls of lost Eden could not have been more beautiful to us; not more awful, round heaven, the walls of sacred Death.

It is not possible to imagine, in any time of the world, a more blessed entrance into life, for a chid of such a temperament as mine. True, the temperament belonged to the age: a very few years – within the hundred – before that, no child could have been born to care for mountains, or for the men that lived among them, in that way. Till Rousseau's time, there had been no 'sentimental' love of nature . . . The sight of the Alps was not only the revelation of the beauty of the earth, but the opening of the first page of its volume – I went down that evening from the garden-terrace of Schaffhausen with my destiny fixed. (35.115–16)

In relating this and other crucial experiences, Ruskin, like so many Victorians, including Carlyle, Tennyson, and Mill, employed the pattern of a religious-conversion narrative. *Praeterita*, though it does present climactic moments, does not, like most conversion narratives, build towards a single climax or moment of illumination. Rather Ruskin organizes his materials into a series of climactic illuminations, such as that attained by drawing the ivy and the aspen, each of which can stand to some extent by itself. I write 'to some extent' because each moment of vision, each new perception, does join to others in a sequence to form a whole greater than the sum of individual parts. Nonc the less, his primary organization is around centres or moments of personally achieved vision, each of which is accommodated within a segment, a fragment. In other words, *Praeterita*, relies upon the same structural principles that inform *Modern Painters*, *The Stones of Venice*, and his other major works.

Such a recognition helps explain how *Praeterita*, although incomplete, can be one of the greatest of autobiographies. Specifically, it explains how an unfinished work deliberately written in a fragmented manner creates such powerful effects. Such a recognition also leads to a better understanding of a peculiar form of narrative technique – or possibly of an entire genre – which provides a sense of aesthetic completeness and rhetorical effectiveness, even though it apparently lacks the formal completeness of narrative.

Thackeray's daughter thought Ruskin's portraits in language so brilliant that she believed he should have been a novelist – a point that brings to the fore the nature of narrative and Ruskin's structures of interpretation. The problem, at least as Ruskin saw it, was that he could not relate a story effectively, and one way of looking at *Praeterita* is as an alternative to conventional narrative, to which he did not feel himself particularly suited. This is no confession of major weakness since genuis always builds upon its limitations. Tennyson, for example, did not have much of a gift for conventional narrative structure either, so he developed a poetic form in *In Memoriam* and *The Idylls of the King* which avoided it, relying instead upon complex interweaving of juxtaposed climactic moments, visions, and dreams. In doing so, this supposedly conservative poet managed to create the kind of narrative mode for which Conrad, Faulkner, and Woolf generally receive credit in histories of the novel. *Praeterita*, which had such a major influence on Proust, relies upon a similar, if more diffuse, narrative mode. By organizing his 'visionary flowers', as he called them, into a series of self-sufficient narratives, Ruskin created a literary form that proceeds by juxtaposition and accumulation more than by narrative progressions.

Of course, Ruskin settled upon such a literary structure, to which he was so temperamentally inclined, because he believed conventional narrative falsified the kind of tale he wished to relate. According to him, the complexity of history necessarily conflicts with the simplifying tendencies of narrative: 'Whether in the biography of a nation, or of a single person, it is alike impossible to trace it steadily through successive years. Some forces are failing while others strengthen, and most act irregularly, or else at uncorresponding periods of renewed enthusiasm after intervals of lassitude. For all clearness of exposition, it is necessary to follow first one, then another, without confusing notices of what is happening in other directions' (35.169).

Essentially, Ruskin's literary structure organizes the work itself and the reader's perception of it into discrete yet individually satisfying segments or episodes. This description of Ruskin's characteristic literary structure strikes a familiar note with readers of his other works. The five volumes of *Modern Painters* and the many numbers of *Fors Clavigera* share the segmented, episodic, and yet strangely satisfying structure of the autobiography. All these works progress by means of a series of illuminations, moments of vision, and epiphanies.

Ruskin saw his own experiences as taking the form of a pattern of loss and gain. The losses include time lost, but more importantly, people lost, for this gentle memory fugue contains an astonishing number of deaths and death-bed scenes. The gains, the recompense for all this personal loss, occur almost entirely in terms of vision, in learning to see things correctly, whatever the cost, whatever the pain. Another way of putting this point would be to refer to his repeated emphases upon Paradise, earthly edens, and paradises lost which appear throughout this autobiography. Autobiographers frequently organize their experiences, thereby giving them order and meaning, in terms of central metaphors, images, or analogies. Ruskin, one of the most metaphorical of writers, uses many such chains of analogy to interpret his past experience, but the dominant one in *Praeterita* consists of a series of juxtaposed lost edens and Pisgah Sights.

Although Ruskin's autobiography, like the autobiographcal elements in his other writings, draws upon the literature of religious conversion for image, rhetoric, and structure, it differs from it in an important way. For it does not attempt merely to testify to the experience of spiritual, aesthetic, or political truth; it tries, instead, to make the reader re-experience something of crucial importance to Ruskin by placing him, as it were, inside Ruskin's consciousness. Ruskin's autobiographical prose, like his art criticism, thus fulfils his own frequently stated requirements for imaginative art. According to him, we recall, great art and literature provided an essential means of enabling the audience to share the emotions and imagination of the artist and poet. To enable the audience to share his past, he relies upon a literature of experience, upon a kind of literature whose primary rhetorical strategy is to make the reader experience his feelings, thoughts, and reasonings. *Praeterita*, like *In Memoriam*, uses its data primarily for an imaginative, emotional effect. Each argument encountered, each person experienced, each landscape confronted is a stage of experience, a rung on the ladder of a developing and liberating vision. The costs of attaining that almost unique vision were great, and one of them was that he became too much a creature of the eye, that is, too much a being who lives isolated and apart and lives only in what he sees.

Therefore, when the world of *Praeterita* appears at Ruskin's bidding, he does not raise a curtain and have us observe a continuing series of happenings. Instead, he takes us by the arm and shows us a gallery of pictures. One picture suggests comparison with another, we move back and forth; and whether or not we arrive at the end of the gallery, we have a sense of being with Ruskin, the spectator of his own life.

Conclusion

The unifying factor in Ruskin's writings, as we have seen, appears in his career-long drive to interpret matters for his contemporaries. The interpretations of painting and architecture with which he began his career met with early and lasting success. Drawing upon the rhetoric and techniques of the Victorian preacher, Wordsworthian conceptions of the poet, and Neoclassical theories of painting and the beautiful, Ruskin offered his Victorian audience convincing arguments for the essential earnestness, the relevance and moral importance, of the visual arts. Arguments of this kind couched in this kind of language were what his contemporaries wanted to hear. As early as 1851, which was only nine years after the publication of *Modern Painters I*, Ruskin began to emphasize the political dimensions of art, and although *The Stones of Venice* was well received, a large part of his audience was disturbed by his touching upon such matters. This was not the kind of argument many wished to hear stated in any kind of language, and the objections to his ideas increased with *Unto This Last* (1862) as reviewers found his eminently sane views of society 'mad' and dangerous.

Although the sense of isolation that Ruskin seems to have felt in varying degrees throughout his life certainly increased after 1860 (which was also the period during which he abandoned his childhood religion), he still retained an audience for his political lectures and publications. Indeed, having disbursed much of the fortune he inherited after his father died in 1864, he earned enough money from his books, including those on political economy, to remain a wealthy man. One of the reasons that Ruskin thus continued to be a popular, if controversial, author lies in the fact that he gradually gained a new audience, one composed of members of the working classes, to supplement and in some cases replace his earlier one.

Ruskin did not, however, concentrate entirely upon political economy in his mid and late career, for he continued his Oxford lectures and published on subjects ranging from ornithology and botany to painting and air pollution. Beginning in 1878, bouts of mental illness intermittently incapacitated him, but during his calm periods he wrote some of his finest work, including *The Art of England* and *Praeterita*. Ruskin's last acts of interpretation centre upon his own life in *Praeterita*, a quiet, beautiful, lyrical work written during periods when his mind and spirit were calm. After 1888, such moments of peace became ever rarer, and Ruskin remained isolated at Brantwood. Ironically, just at the time when thousands of readers in England and abroad received the words of Ruskin the prophet with adulation, he himself could take no solace from that fact.

As recent histories of literature, art, architecture, design, and political theory make clear, we are just beginning to perceive the degree to which John Ruskin, Interpreter, influenced his own age and continues to affect ours. Ruskin, however, possesses more than historical importance. He remains England's great art critic, and his magnificent prose still teaches us to see and to see better. His social criticism, with its constant emphasis that we can understand our lives, remains immediate and relevant, as does his insistence that the chief test of theories of art, society, and politics is the question, Do they enhance life and spirit, do they make us more fully, more richly, alive?

Further reading

Writings by Ruskin

Students of Ruskin's life and work are indebted to the Library Edition of the *Works*, ed. E. T. Cook and Alexander Wedderburn, 39 vols. (George Allen, London, 1903–12), which contains invaluable background, biographical, and bibliographical information and reproduces as well many of Ruskin's drawings. The *Works* must be supplemented by the poorly edited *Diaries of John Ruskin*, ed. Joan Evans and J. H. Whitehouse, 3 vols. (Clarendon Press, Oxford, 1956), and *Brantwood Diary of John Ruskin*, ed. Helen Gill Viljoen (Yale University Press, New Haven, 1971).

Cook and Wedderburn include a selection of letters in Volumes 36 and 37 and in the introductions to other volumes, but no complete edition of the correspondence exists. The more important published portions include *Ruskin's Letters from Venice, 1851–1852*, ed. John L. Bradley (Yale University Press, New Haven, 1955); *The Winnington Letters*, ed. Van Akin Burd (Harvard University Press, Cambridge, Mass., 1969); *Ruskin in Italy: Letters to His Parents 1845*, ed. Harold I. Shapiro (Clarendon Press, Oxford, 1972); *The Ruskin Family Letters: The Correspondence of John James Ruskin, His Wife, and His Son, 1801–1843*, ed. Van Akin Burd, 2 vols. (Cornell University Press, Ithaca, 1973); and '*Your Good Influence On Me': The Correspondence of John Ruskin and William Holman Hunt*, ed. George P. Landow (Rylands Library, Manchester, 1977).

Writings about Ruskin

The long period during which students of art, literature, and politics generally ignored Ruskin ended more than a decade ago with a flurry of of editions, biographies, and critical studies. The chapter on Ruskin by Francis Townsend in *Victorian Non-Fiction: A Guide to Research*, ed. David J. DeLaura (Modern Language Association, New York, 1977), provides valuable summary judgements of both primary and secondary materials, and the annual bibliographical issue of *Victorian Studies* lists current books and articles and notes reviews of recent books. Readers may also wish to consult *The Ruskin Newsletter*, which contains notices of current sales of Ruskiniana as well as of other matters of interest to students of his life, art, writing, and influence.

Derrick Leon, *Ruskin The Great Victorian* (Routledge & Kegan Paul, London, 1949), remains the best biography, although two useful ones have recently appeared: Joan Abse, *John Ruskin the Passionate Moralist* (Knopf, New York, 1982), and J. D. Hunt, *The Wider Sea: A Life of John Ruskin* (Viking, New York, 1982).

John D. Rosenberg, *The Darkening Glass: A Portrait of Ruskin's Genius* (Columbia University Press, New York, 1961), a pioneering study that is responsible for much of the current interest in Ruskin, has been superseded by more recent work but still contains many valuable insights, as does Robert Hewison, *John Ruskin or the Argument of the Eye* (Thames and Hudson, London, 1975). Two of the most important studies of Ruskin during the past decade are Elizabeth K. Helsinger's *Ruskin and the Art of the Beholder* (Harvard University Press, Cambridge, Mass., 1982), and Paul Sawyer's *Ruskin's Poetic Argument: The Design of His Major Works* (Cornell University Press, Ithaca, 1985). George P. Landow, *The Aesthetic and Critical Theories of John Ruskin* (Princeton University Press, Princeton, 1971), and Paul H. Walton, *The Drawings of John Ruskin* (Clarendon Press, Oxford, 1972), provide specialized discussions of his thought within the context of Victorian and earlier ideas. Walton's volume, which contains many reproductions of Ruskin's drawings and water-colours, sets his pictures against the background of eighteenth- and nineteenth-century drawing treatises. Landow, who examines the sources and development of Ruskin's conceptions of beauty and the arts, shows how he formulated a Victorian aesthetic by drawing upon Neoclassical conceptions of painting, beauty, sublimity, and picturesqueness and combining them with Romantic conceptions of poetry and evangelical attitudes towards interpretation. James Clarke Sherburne, *John Ruskin, or the Ambiguities of Abundance: A Study in Social and Economic Criticism* (Harvard University Press, Cambridge, Mass., 1972), an essential book, examines the sources, evolution, and influence of his political economy. Raymond E. Fitch, *The Poison Sky: Myth and Apocalypse in Ruskin* (Ohio University Press, Athens, Ohio, 1982) provides a massive study of the subjects covered in its title. *New Approaches to Ruskin*, ed. Robert Hewison (Routledge & Kegan Paul, London, 1982), which contains important essays on individual works, provides a valuable survey of the state of current Ruskin criticism and scholarship.

The study of Ruskin's influence on the arts has produced some interesting results, but much more work needs to be done in this area. Roger B. Stein, *Ruskin and Aesthetic Thought in America, 1840–1900* (Harvard University Press, Cambridge, Mass., 1967) offers a pioneering survey of its broad subject, while Kristine O. Garrigan, *Ruskin on Architecture: His Thought and Influence* (University of Wisconsin Press, Madison, 1973); Eve Blau, *Ruskinian Gothic* (Princeton University Press, Princeton, 1982), and George L. Hersey, *High Victorian Gothic: A Study in Associationism* (Johns Hopkins University Press, Baltimore, 1972), contain much valuable information about his influence on architecture. Allen Staley, *The Pre-Raphaelite Landscape* (Clarendon Press, Oxford, 1973), and George P. Landow, *William Holman Hunt and Typological Symbolism* (Yale University Press, New Haven and London, 1979), examine his influence upon different aspects of Pre-Raphaelitism, as does Robert Secor, *John Ruskin and Alfred Hunt: New Letters and the Record of a Friendship*, English Literary Studies Monograph Studies No. 25 (University of Victoria Press, Victoria, B. C., 1982).

A Ruskin chronology

1819   John Ruskin is born in London on 8 February to John James and Margaret Cox Ruskin.

1836   Resides in Oxford, accompanied by his mother, until 1840. Publishes a series of articles entitled 'The Poetry of Architecture' in the *Architectural Magazine* (1837–8).

1839   Wins the Newdigate Prize for poetry at Oxford with *Salsette and Elephanta*. Meets Wordsworth.

1840   First meets Turner. Falls ill, possibly with consumption, and leaves Oxford for a foreign tour with parents which lasts from September until June. Meets Georgianna Tollemache, later Lady Mount-Temple, who remains one of his closest friends.

1841   Writes *The King of the Golden River* for Euphemia Chalmers Gray, whom he marries in 1848.

1842   Takes BA at Oxford and abandons idea of taking holy orders. Begins *Modern Painters*.

1843   Publishes first volume of *Modern Painters* anonymously in May.

1844   Revises *Modern Painters I*, deleting much of its polemics. Reads A. F. Rio's *La Poésie de l'art chrétienne* and continues studies of botany and geology. Purchases Turner's *The Slave Ship*.

1846   Publishes *Modern Painters*, Volume II, which marks a new departure in his thought.

1847   Reviews Lord Lindsay's *Sketches of the History of Christian Art* in the June *Quarterly Review*. Unknown to Ruskin, *Modern Painters II* inspires William Holman Hunt, John Everett Millais, and Dante Gabriel Rossetti to emulate Tintoretto's fusions of visual realism and elaborate symbolism.

1848   Marries Euphemia Chalmers Gray, a distant cousin, on 10 April, after which he and his wife tour Normandy. Studies Gothic architecture.

1849   Publishes *The Seven Lamps of Architecture*. Works in Venice studying the city's architecture and history from November until March 1850.

1850   Publishes collected *Poems* and *The King of the Golden River*, which is, however, dated the following year.

1851   Publishes the first volume of *The Stones of Venice*, 'Notes on the Construction of Sheepfolds', and *Pre-Raphaelitism*. Defends Hunt and Millais in letters to *The Times* after Coventry Patmore points out their work to him. Meets Millais, Rossetti, Hunt, and other members of the Pre-Raphaelite circle. Works in Venice from September until June 1852 on *The Stones of Venice*. Turner dies, having made Ruskin a trustee of his will.

1853   The second and third volumes of *The Stones of Venice* are published. Travels with wife, Millais, and Millais's brother in Scottish Highlands.

1854   Marriage annulled on grounds of non-consummation. (The following year Effie marries Millais.) Begins lecturing on art at the newly founded Working Men's College and becomes friendly with D. G. Rossetti and Elizabeth Siddall. Writes letters to *The Times* defending Pre-Raphaelite painting. Publishes *Lectures on Art and Architecture* delivered in Edinburgh the previous year.

1855   Begins *Academy Notes*, annual reviews of the June Royal Academy exhibition which continue until 1859 (with a single issue in 1875). Meets Tennyson.

1856   Publishes the third and fourth volumes of *Modern Painters*, which concern the rise of Romantic art and attitudes towards landscape. Meets Charles Eliot Norton, his American friend, disciple, and popularizer.

1857 Publishes *The Elements of Drawing* and *The Political Economy of Art*. Lectures extensively and studies works in Turner bequest.

1858 Meets and falls in love with Rose La Touche. Decisively abandons his Protestant religious faith in Turin.

1860 Completes the final volume of *Modern Painters* and publishes political and social criticism in the *Cornhill Magazine*, but protests by readers prompt Thackeray, the editor, to limit Ruskin to four articles later published as *Unto This Last* (1862).

1862 Publishes 'Essays on Political Economy' in *Fraser's Magazine* (1862–3); these are published in book form as *Munera Pulveris* in 1872.

1864 Ruskin's father dies on 2 March and leaves him considerable wealth. Writes and delivers 'Traffic' and 'Of King's Treasuries'.

1865 Publishes *Sesame and Lilies*.

1866 Publishes *The Crown of Wild Olive* and *The Ethics of the Dust*, this last work a series of dialogues with children explaining geology based upon his occasional teaching at the Winnington School. Ruskin's proposal of marriage to Rose La Touche begins a decade of frustration and emotional turmoil.

1867 Publishes *Time and Tide*, letters to a British labourer about social and political issues. Becomes friendly with the social worker Octavia Hill.

1869 Publishes *The Queen of the Air*, a study of Greek myth which expands ideas found in the closing volumes of *Modern Painters*. Appointed the first Slade Professor of Fine Art at Oxford.

1871 Purchases Brantwood near Coniston in the Lake District from the radical W. J. Linton. Undertakes social experiments including street sweeping in London and road mending in Oxford. Begins publication of *Fors Clavigera*, which continues in monthly parts until

1878, after which it appears intermittently. Is seriously ill, with mental and physical illnesses, at Matlock. Mother dies 5 December.

1875 Rose dies, insane, at age twenty-seven.

1878 Founds the Guild of St. George. Suspends *Fors* after an attack of madness in the spring and is unable to testify in *Whistler v. Ruskin* in November.

1879 Resigns Slade Professorship at Oxford, in large part because of *Whistler v. Ruskin.*

1880 Recovering from attacks of madness, he resumes *Fors* and begins 'Fiction, Fair and Foul', a series that appears intermittently in the *Nineteenth Century* until October 1881. Publishes *A Joy For Ever*, an expanded version of *The Political Economy of Art* (1857).

1883 Resumes Professorship at Oxford after re-election and lectures on *The Art of England*, which contains extensive comments on Hunt, Rossetti, Burne-Jones, and other Victorian artists.

1884 Delivers 'The Storm-Cloud of the Nineteenth Century' as a lecture at the London Institution and begins to publish the Oxford lectures entitled *The Pleasures of England*. Publishes *The Art of England* in book form. Frequently experiences mental turmoil.

1885 Continues publication of *The Pleasures of England* and publishes *Praeterita*, his autobiography, which appeared intermittently in parts until July 1889. Mental illness forces temporary cessation of writing.

1886 Suffers attacks of mental illness.

1900 Dies of influenza on 20 January and is buried in Coniston churchyard.

Index

Index

Pre-Raphaelites, the, 2, 4, 24, 42–3
prophecy, biblical, 8
Proust, Marcel, 84
Prout, Samuel, 78
Pugin, Augustus Welby Northmore, 10

Raphael (Raffaello Sanzio), 27–8, 82
Reynolds, Sir Joshua, 7, 9, 13, 26–7
Ricardo, David, 16
Richmond, George, 77
Ritchie, Anne Thackeray, 84
Rogers, Samuel, 77
Romanticism, 9–10, 13
Rosa, Salvator, 15
Rossetti, Dante Gabriel, 39, 43
Rousseau, Jean Jacques, 73
Rubens, Peter Paul, 77–8
Runciman, Charles, 77
Ruskin, Euphemia (Effie) Chalmers Gray, 2
Ruskin, John, abandons religious belief, 2, 49; alternation of vision and satire, 39–41; and evangelical preaching, 10; on the grotesque, 4, 45–8; and Italian Primitives, 4; as spectator, 78–9; as Victorian sage, 16–17, 35, 64–5, 68; cinematic prose, 32–3; compositional analyses, 15, 43; consumerist ethic of, 12; creator of a Victorian aesthetic, 9; division of art into symbolic and imitative, 13; dramatizes process of interpretation, 55; eclecticism, 7; evangelical vocabulary, 7; inconsistency, 23; influence of, 4–5, 10; insanity, 3; marriage annulled, 2; parables of

perception, 17–18; Pathetic Fallacy, 14; political beliefs, 16; Slade Professor of Fine Art, 3; teaches at Working Men's College, 2; theories of beauty, 9, 21–2; theories of composition, 15; theories of imagination, 8; timeliness of, 6; visual orientation 21; wins Newdigate Prize, 1

WRITINGS:
A Joy For Ever, 26, 28–9, 61
Academy Notes, 2
Art of England, The, 3, 88
Crown of Wild Olive, The, 2, 8, 15
Elements of Drawing, The, 2, 29
Elements of Perspective, The, 2
Ethics of the Dust, The, 2
Fors Clavigera, 3, 15, 20, 64, 74–5
Harbours of England, The, 2
King of the Golden River, The, 2
Modern Painters, 2, 16, 18–19, 22, 36, 44, 65–6
Modern Painters, Volume I, 17, 22–3, 29–30, 33, 35–7, 40–1, 43, 87
Modern Painters, Volume II, 8–9, 23, 41–2, 48–50
Modern Painters, Volume III, 13–14, 18, 25–7, 44–5, 48–50, 55–6
Modern Painters, Volume IV, 13–14, 18, 48, 50–7
Modern Painters, Volume V, 2, 14–15, 39, 48, 50–7, 60
Munera Pulveris, 2, 15
On the Opening of the Crystal Palace, 61
'On Skiddaw and Derwent Water', 1

98

DATE DUE

MAR 23 '93			
GAYLORD			PRINTED IN U.S.A.